Praise for Ellen D

The Enchanted Cat

2007 COVR AWARD WINNER
Best Book Magick/Shamanism Category

Cottage Witchery

"This is the perfect book to have around
if you want to make every area of
your home magical."—*NewWitch*

Herb Magic for Beginners

"A delightful little book."—Herb *Quarterly*

Garden Witch's Herbal

"A refreshing change from other garden-
variety horticulture books…entertaining
as well as informative."—*New Age Retailer*

Elements of Witchcraft

"[Dugan's] wise-woman tone and gentle
guidance will help nurture budding
natural witches, and her well-written text
will guide novices in their discoveries
as well."—*School Library Journal*

Natural Witchery

"Interspersed throughout the text are lively anecdotes from Dugan's own Samantha Stephens-esque household. The value of this book lies in the warm, personal touch Dugan uses both in her writing and in her craft."—*Publishers Weekly*

"This book is eminently useful. Dugan's voice is engaging and her work is practical and fun."—*PanGaia*

"A gold mine of concepts and resources for the novice to intermediate practitioner… Chock-full of relevant wisdom and lively humor."—*Library Journal*

Practical Prosperity Magick

 CRAFTING SUCCESS
& ABUNDANCE

About the Author

Ellen Dugan is an award-winning author and psychic-clairvoyant who has been a practicing Witch for thirty years. She is high priestess of a mixed magick tradition coven in the St. Louis area. She gardens and practices her Craft in Missouri, where she lives with her family. Also known as the Garden Witch, she is the author of many Llewellyn books, including *Garden Witchery*, *Cottage Witchery*, *Natural Witchery*, and *Garden Witch's Herbal*. Ellen is also an experienced lecturer on a variety of topics, including tarot, psychometry, Witchcraft, and enchanted gardens.

Practical Prosperity Magick

 CRAFTING SUCCESS & ABUNDANCE

Ellen Dugan

LLEWELLYN PUBLICATIONS
Woodbury, Minnesota

FIRST EDITION
Fifth Printing, 2019

Book design and editing by Rebecca Zins
Cover art from iStockphoto.com/000009017108/naphtalina
Cover design by Lisa Novak
Fourth Pentacle of Jupiter by Llewellyn Art Department
Interior graphic element from *1500 Decorative Ornaments*
CD-ROM & *Book* (Dover Publications, 1995)
Tarot images from *Witches Tarot* by Ellen Dugan; illustrated by Mark Evans

Llewellyn is a registered trademark of Llewellyn Worldwide Ltd.

Library of Congress Cataloging-in-Publication Data
Dugan, Ellen, 1963–
  Practical prosperity magick : crafting success & abundance / Ellen Dugan.
    pages   cm
  Includes bibliographical references and index.
  ISBN 978-0-7387-3696-9
  1. Magic. 2. Finance, Personal—Miscellanea. 3. Wealth—Miscellanea.
  4. Success—Miscellanea. I. Title.
  BF1623.F55D84 2014
  133.4'3—dc23

                                                2014004106

Llewellyn Publications
A Division of Llewellyn Worldwide Ltd.
2143 Wooddale Drive
Woodbury, MN 55125-2989
www.llewellyn.com
Printed in the United States of America

To laugh often and much; to win the respect of intelligent people and the affection of children... to leave the world a better place...to know even one life has breathed easier because you have lived. This is to have succeeded.

RALPH WALDO EMERSON

CONTENTS

Water: Letting Prosperity Flow   69

ACKNOWLEDGMENTS

WRITING A BOOK is like embarking on a journey. You think you know where it will take you and what to expect, but often the reality is very different from what you envisioned. The journey can bring frustration, but there is also a chance for wonderful surprises and personal lessons.

I would like to thank the friends who kindly shared information and offered support while I was on this particular journey: Charlynn, Chris, Christopher, Clyde, Dawn, Ember, Ethan, Heather, Jeanne, Jennifer M., Robbie, Sarah, and Tess.

Thanks also to my trainer, Aaron, a soft-spoken young man who challenged me while smiling and who has taught me that success is possible in all areas of your life—even physical fitness. All you have to do is be willing to sweat and work hard.

A few words of appreciation to my editor, Rebecca Zins, and to the team up at Llewellyn: Elysia Gallo, Bill Krause, and Carl and Sandra Weschcke.

Finally, with love to my husband, Ken, and our three children, Kraig, Kyle, and Erin. Thanks for always supporting me and, most of all, for believing that I can do anything I set my mind to. Love ya!

INTRODUCTION

All prosperity begins in the mind and is
dependent only on the full use of
our creative imagination.
RUTH ROSS

HOW DID THIS practical book on prosperity magick come to be? Well, our story begins a few years ago with one frustrated and annoyed Witch getting out of the house to take a break by checking out seasonal Halloween decorations. I was aggravated at yet another delay with a writing project, and in order to preserve what was left of my sanity, I had decided that a change of scenery was called for. As it was early September, I knew that the stores would be chock-full of fun seasonal decorations. With thoughts of my family's upcoming annual gothic Halloween party, I went to the store to check out the Halloween décor—just to look and cheer myself up.

That year in particular had been a tough one financially for my family. My husband had been laid off for six months, and the savings I had so carefully put away for taxes was wiped out to pay for little things like the mortgage, health insurance, the car payment, and groceries. My husband had finally found a new job with good benefits a few months prior, but he (like so many others in this economy) had to take a large pay cut. Money at home was beyond tight, and I had started to think that I might need to go out and look for a part-time seasonal job after my book tour was over in late October.

With out-of-state events looming in my schedule, I could not imagine a prospective employer being willing to work around an employee who could not work most weekends. Also, I had been writing full time for the past seven years; it's a little tough to get a job when you've been out of the workforce for that long—and then there was the whole "well-known author who is a Witch" thing…

I decided that my best course of action was to promote my online classes. A few months prior I had opened up a little online shop selling our handmade pentacles and jewelry. They had done well for us. I remember pushing away from my computer desk at home that day in September and deciding that, since it was a Thursday and a waxing moon, it would be a great time to do a quick little prosperity spell. I knew my husband would be on board for it, so I included him as well.

In my mind I thought the spell would increase online class sales and we would acquire more wholesale orders for the pentacles, and that maybe the magick would snag my husband a pay raise. I quickly gathered my herbs from the garden, rounded up my supplies, and started composing a spell verse in my mind. I set up a seven-day candle with corresponding crystals and the fresh herbs. I tucked a recent pay stub from my husband's new job into the setup, added one of our handmade pentacles and a class transcript, and got ready to cast.

As I was worried about our finances and impatient to get the spell rolling, I worked my magick quickly. I recall vividly that I said, "I am willing to work for the money, Goddess—whatever it takes to improve the money situation so we can catch up on these bills."

I finished the spell and cleaned up. I tucked the stones, crystals, and then the jar candle inside of my large cast-iron cauldron—where the candle could safely burn for the next seven days—and patted myself on the back.

See? Simple, quick, and easy. All done, and now it was time to go window shopping.

As I drove to the store, Tess, an author friend of mine, called me. We chatted about energy and magick, and I told her how I felt a bit stuck these past few months. Then, as I pulled into the store's parking lot, she asked how the current delayed project was going, and I unloaded.

Bless her heart, she listened to me complain about the delays and dramas, then quietly said that she felt an entire change of scenery was called for. I laughed as I climbed out of the car. Lugging my purse and still talking on my cell phone, I remarked that with Samhain being around the corner, I was looking to change the scenery into something more gothic and dramatic.

I breezed into the store and headed for the Halloween decorations, enjoying my chat with Tess as I perused the displays. She suggested I start a new book project—something different—and I brushed that suggestion aside; I had my hands full as it was. (I should have listened to her. She's a wise woman, that Tess.) But she cheered me up and made me laugh at myself. I felt so much lighter after talking to her.

I put my phone away, mood lightened, and then found a hilarious "Witch & Famous" sign that was half price. It was so snarky and cute that I thought it would be funny to hang in my home office year-round. I picked it up and headed for the checkout counter. As I walked through the store, I ran into a friend of my daughter's.

"Hey, Ellen!" she said as she popped out from around an endcap. I have known Amelia since she and my daughter, Erin, were in elementary school together. I refused to think about how old that made me.

"Well, hey!" I gave her a hug and reminded myself that these days Amelia, a recent college graduate, was one of the managers at this store.

"I heard you talking on your cell phone." Amelia winked at me.

Oh, hell. I *had* kept my voice down. No, really—I can do that.

I wondered if somebody had heard me talking about Witch stuff and freaked? Nope; apparently Amelia had been following me around the store for a bit, wanting to talk to me, but waited until I had finished my conversation.

"Are you still a floral designer?" Amelia asked.

Confused by the question, I answered, "Well, yes. I will always be a floral designer. Why?"

Amelia explained that the store was in desperate need of one. The current designer was going on maternity leave in mid-November and would only be coming back part-time. All of the managers had been told to be on the lookout for a designer, so when Amelia saw me, she pounced.

I explained about the tour dates throughout the month of October. Amelia assured me that this would not be a problem as the other designer was not leaving until the middle of November. I tried to tell her that I didn't think it would be a good idea... She told me to fill out an application online and to call her and let her know once it was in the system.

Amelia had me program her cell phone number into my phone, and I left the store and thought about it. Filling in for another woman about to go on maternity leave made me a bit nervous; I figured the job would be temporary. I did not want to work full time with several book projects going on, but I guessed that during late November and December, while the other designer was on maternity leave, it would be close to forty hours a week.

When I returned home, the first thing that caught my eye was the large stack of bills in the mailbox. My stomach sank. Then I saw my calico cat, Brianna, sitting on our brick hearth next to the cauldron. I could see the spell candle flickering away, and with a jolt I heard my own voice come back to me from the spell I had cast only an hour or so earlier: "Goddess, I am willing to *work* for the money..."

I had to laugh at myself.

What the hell, I decided. So I went online, filled out the application, and sent it in. It certainly couldn't hurt to check it out. I did not have to take the job, I told myself. As a matter of fact, I did not even tell my husband about it.

As promised, I called Amelia and let her know that the application had been filled out. She gleefully told me to expect a phone call and an interview in the next few days. Oh jeez. I stammered and, for once, was at a loss for words.

Two days later I went in for the interview. I explained my tour schedule to the general manager and described what sort of books I wrote. (I figured it was best to put all my cards on the table, so to speak.) The manager brushed that aside, assuring me the job would be three days a week until the other designer left for maternity leave in mid-November. This would be a part-time job, she promised. I was asked to come in and work up a few floral arrangements so they could see what I could do design-wise.

So I went in, met the other floral designer, and worked up a couple of arrangements. I printed out the dates I was unavailable in September and October and gave them to the store manager so they would be on file. I figured they would be a deal breaker, but a few days after that I was offered the job, and at a much better pay rate than I would have imagined. I was informed they would work around my tour dates. No problem. Oh and by the way, could I start that week? They wanted me to work with the other designer for a few months before she went on maternity leave, to help them get ready for the huge amount of holiday arrangements that were needed.

Smugly I congratulated myself on my spellcasting prowess. One quick and simple spellcast, and no waiting for results. Boom! Less than an hour after I cast it, a job offer dropped into my lap…a week later and I was employed.

This prosperity magick stuff was *so* easy…

The Witch Goes Back to Work

*Please remember that your difficulties do not define
you; they simply strengthen your ability to overcome.*

MAYA ANGELOU

For the first month it was a whirlwind, and soon I was working five days a week—which I was not happy about, as the manager had promised me three days a week when I accepted the job. The other designer was a challenge to work with, and it was an uncomfortable atmosphere. The poor thing had absolutely no sense of humor. I was tempted to check her for a pulse a couple of times... There was a definite diva quality to her behavior, and privately I started thinking of her as the pregnant princess. Management certainly treated her that way.

By mid-October I came to the unpleasant realization that the job sucked. I admit that I have no patience for office politics. I only wanted to work part time, do my job, and go home. The majority of the employees were female, and it was a nasty brew of gossip, office politics, competition, and daily dramas at the store. I ignored it as best I could and wondered what in the world I had gotten myself into. Had my spell backfired?

Then I started to have vivid recurring dreams about the princess going into labor early. As I don't often have recurring dreams, especially about folks I don't know well, it made me pay attention. When we rolled closer to the end of October, I told the princess that I felt she would never make it to her mid-November due date. That baby was coming soon—as in before Halloween.

She smirked at me, commented it was nice that I *thought* I was a psychic and all, but whatever. She laughed about it to the management, and I endured a good week of jokes and laughter about the "witch" at work. Shortly thereafter, I was proven right. The baby was born a week before Halloween and over three weeks before its due date. Nobody at work talked to me for days. There was a lot of whispering and folks studying me from afar... It may have had something to do with it being right before Halloween, or it may have been from me rubbing my hands together and cackling occasionally.

Some folks simply have no sense of humor.

The general manager, now that the pregnant princess was on maternity leave, dropped her nice façade, and I soon realized why all the teens and college students who worked at the store were very cautious of her. I remember thinking to myself one horrid afternoon after the manager had been in my face that nobody in their right mind would ever want to work at this store. The atmosphere was toxic, and I hoped the manager would just go away, leave me alone, and let me do my job in peace. I even energetically sent a little nudge toward that outcome.

Damn it. I *know* better than that.

With the stress of the writing projects and working more hours sooner than I had anticipated, I simply did not think—I only reacted. And I believe that the gods were listening because the next day, the store manager tearfully announced that she had to take an unplanned medical leave starting a week before Thanksgiving and would be out for at least six weeks.

I was so relieved. Working retail over the holiday season is always horrible, but working with that manager breathing down my neck would have been ghastly. I also realized very quickly that I should have been more careful with my wishes and energy nudges, but there was nothing I could do about it after the fact.

On the plus side, the atmosphere at work was much better with the manager on leave. I had started taking the pay from all the extra hours I was working and stashing it in my savings. Maybe the original money spell had worked out okay after all? The cash was certainly flowing…

A replacement manager from another store was assigned to us a few days later, and he and I got along very well. I cranked out hundreds of holiday floral designs and told myself to enjoy being creative in a different way with the silk flowers. It was busy, chaotic, and insane. It took me over and I was simply on autopilot: get up, go to work, bust my ass, deal with or dodge store dramas, be polite to insane holiday shoppers, come home, scrape off glitter, and repeat.

When it was time for the replacement manager to go back to his own store, he gave me a hug and his cell phone number, and told me that he would love it if I worked in his store's floral department. When our store manager returned from medical leave in early January, she stormed in, stopped, and glared straight at me. To say she was hostile toward me after her return was an understatement. Hello, karma. *Note to self: watch those wishes and energy nudges, Ellen.*

The mood in the store took a nosedive. Everyone was unhappy with our store manager being back and on a tear. So much for my spellcasting prowess…I had landed a job and brought in some serious cash, but obviously I had done something wrong because I was absolutely miserable for the five months I was an employee at that store.

Turning Mistakes into Success

The first step toward success is taken when
you refuse to be a captive of the environment
in which you first find yourself.

MARK CAINE

I turned in my resignation within two weeks of the cranky store manager's return. What a relief! It took about three days and a lot of energetic cleansing to start feeling like my old self again. I kept at it, scraping off negativity from that job the way I once scraped off holiday glitter.

Still, there was a bright side to the experience. I had brushed up on my floral design skills, and that could come in handy if I ever needed to pick up another seasonal job. I had also caught up on bills *and* had actually managed to put away enough extra money in my savings for my husband and I to fly down to Florida and spend a few days on the beach for our thirtieth wedding anniversary. Bonus!

Also, I had to admit that working in that drama-filled, crazy store gave me plenty to think about when it came to prosperity magick and how it truly manifests. Five months of misery gave me lots of time to look at the situation and figure out where the original spell had gone wrong. I spent my evenings digging through magickal reference material and studying harder than I had in years.

I discovered that effective prosperity magick is so much more than lighting a green candle and asking for money. After almost thirty years of practicing Witchcraft, I had made a major rookie mistake. In my arrogance, I had forgotten something very important about spellwork. My oversight was that I was frustrated, aggravated, and stressed out when I cast the original money spell—which, in turn, brought more frustration, anger, and stress into my life when the magick manifested. How many times have I told other folks to be calm, centered, and business-like while casting their own spells? This is what you call ironic.

That spell had certainly brought money into my life, so on one level it was successful. However, it was unsuccessful on many levels, as it brought more drama, tension, and unhappiness into my world as well. Those crazy five months and that whirlwind turn of events are what really got me to thinking about prosperity magick from a different perspective. Prosperity magick is a perennially favorite topic with Witches and other magick users, and it seems deceptively simple at first—however, it is not.

The more I researched it, the more interesting and layered a topic it seemed to be. I asked myself: How could prosperity magick work more effectively? How could I make it more user-friendly, smarter, safer, and more practical? By carefully examining how this variety of magick manifests, I discovered more of the nuances that can come with this type of spellcasting.

And what do you know? It *is* deeper and more complex than I ever imagined. Just doing an "I need money" spell without thinking about those nuances may land you a job, but it can also bring chaos and anxiety into your world—especially if you are not thoughtful and deliberate with your prosperity spellcasting. You need to be practical, and you need to *really* understand just what it is that you are inviting into your life on an energetic level.

What You Will Find in This Book

Books can be dangerous. The best ones should
be labeled "This could change your life."

HELEN EXLEY

If you want to learn how to correctly work magick for positive change and to bring prosperity into your life, then this is the book for you. This book does indeed have spells, charms, and rituals, but it also has the foundational material that you will need to understand prosperity and abundance magick and all of its degrees and complexities.

To begin, we will use the framework of the four natural elements to explore the topic. In the first chapter, which aligns with the element of earth, we will explore the foundations and fundamentals of magick. We will tackle the seven Hermetic laws from a down-to-earth perspective and explore the law of attraction. The elements of spellwork and ritual are here for you to build upon, providing you with a strong foundation from which to advance your prosperity magick studies.

Then we will look at the other natural elements and learn how they apply to prosperity magick and how their energies combine and enhance your prosperity work and your attitude. We will explore happiness and success, motivation and transformation, wealth and the magick of manifestation. There will be chapters on good luck charms, talismans, coin magick, and attracting abundance, as well as a chapter on removing obstacles to your success. You will discover how to solve common magickal snafus and what your personal magickal energy, or PME, is. There are chapters on herb and crystal magick, with a bountiful amount of new prosperity and success spells for you to try throughout. Plus there is information on planetary magick, theurgy and thaumaturgy, and deities that correspond with prosperity and abundance. You will discover spells for the solitary Witch as well as a prosperity ritual you can work with your coven or group. To wrap it up, there are also two appendices, both pertaining to prosperity work.

There is plenty of practical magick for you to work with here. If you are ready to advance your Craft and expand your magickal skills, you have come to the right place. *Practical Prosperity Magick* can help to correctly bring success and abundance into your world with smart and smoothly manifesting magick that improves the quality of your life. Let me show you how.

Chapter One

EARTH:
FOUNDATIONS &
FUNDAMENTAL KNOWLEDGE

*Man must feel the earth to know himself
and recognize his values...*
CHARLES LINDBERGH

THE ELEMENT OF earth provides us with stability, riches, and a strong, sturdy foundation, which allows us to build upon this base and add to our knowledge of magick in general. The element of earth is complementary to practical magick and prosperity magick in particular.

When you work magick for success and prosperity, typically this does not mean that money will just fall into your lap. As I wrote about in the introduction, an opportunity for a job literally fell into mine within an hour after I cast that quick spell. However, I still had to follow the steps and apply for the position, set up the interviews, and so forth. Then I had to live and work with the negative consequences of my attitude and my emotions that I was experiencing when I originally cast the spell.

A real problem begins when you don't stop to consider what mood and emotions you are bringing into your spellwork. In my hurry to cast a quick spell, I overlooked the deeper laws that magick is founded upon. There are some important fundamentals that many magick users may neglect in their rush to work spells. It can happen to anyone—even those of us who have been doing this for three decades. Ahem.

The point here is to step up and reacquaint yourself with these foundational principles. It is well worth your time, and it helps to keep your magick on track and energetically correct. In reality, the *flash boom!* of a quickly manifested spell is impressive, but you're actually better off with a spell that unfolds gently and smoothly, thus creating that positive change you desired with far less drama. This fundamental knowledge is important, as it lays the foundation that you will build upon. By understanding exactly how magick works and the science behind the Craft, these principles will help you to gain control over your spellwork.

Hermes Trismegistus and the Hermetic Principles

Transmute yourself from dead stones
into living philosophical stones.

GERHARDT DORN

Truth be told, a lot of magick is founded on philosophy. Case in point: the Hermetic principles. The Hermetic principles are a set of philosophical beliefs based upon the ancient writings of Hermes Trismegistus. According to folklore, these principles or laws were originally inscribed upon emerald tablets and were discovered by Alexander the Great when he opened Hermes Trismegistus's tomb. After the tablets were translated, they were supposedly hidden again; however, the wisdom obtained from the tablets was carefully protected and handed down over the ages. For example, one of the more well-known lines on the tablets may look familiar to today's magickal practitioners: "As above, so below. As within, so without." The legend of the tablets became the cornerstone for Hermetic sciences and philosophy. These ancient principles laid the foundation for alchemy and ceremonial magick.

Some attribute this philosophy to the actual writings of the god Hermes and others say it was the Egyptian god Thoth. There are some schools of thought that believe it was *both* gods—that Hermes was and is a god of magick and knowledge, and thus is known by many different cultures and by many different names. There is also another popular theory that says Hermes Trismegistus was a divine teacher/alchemist/ master magician of sorts. Or that "he," the author of the principles, was really a trio of anonymous initiates…confused yet?

Well, for starters, try breaking down the meaning of Hermes Trismegistus's name. *Hermetic* means "sealed" or, some say, "secret knowledge," while *Trismegistus* means "thrice great" and refers to the three branches of wisdom that Hermes Trismegistus possessed.

The first branch of wisdom Hermes Trismegistus possessed was alchemy. This was not so much the physical act of turning lead into gold (which creates a philosopher's stone); instead, this alchemy was more of a focus on the transformation of the self, of the soul.

The second branch of his wisdom was astrology. The Hermetic philosophers believed that while astrology has influences on the earth, it does not control our actions. Wisdom was to be gained by knowing and understanding these influences and how best to deal with their effects.

Finally, the third branch of Hermes Trismegistus's wisdom was theurgy: magick or miracles performed with the aid of a beneficial spirit, god, or angel, or what we would consider "high magick" today.

This information was anonymously published in 1908 in French. It was later published in 1912 in English. This book was called *The Kybalion*, and it was written by "three initiates" who, legend has it, were secret Hermetic philosophers. Interestingly enough, the work inside the book is, in fact, dedicated to Hermes Trismegistus.

Hermes Trismegistus is a familiar archetypal image to most modern-day magickal practitioners; you just may not have realized that you have seen him. However, he will be very familiar to you if you own a tarot deck. The major arcana tarot card titled the Magician is rumored to represent Hermes Trismegistus himself. Look at how the magician in the card points both to the ground and to the sky. This is a classic demonstration of the Hermetic phrase "As above, so below."

The Magician card from Witches Tarot

It seems to me like old Hermes Trismegistus is everywhere. Not only is he looking out at us from the major arcana of the tarot deck, but he is also found within the heart of every magician and Witch, patiently waiting for us to open our eyes and become reacquainted with him, embracing his magickal lessons and ways.

Wrapping Your Mind Around the Hermetic Principles

*I have never let my schooling
interfere with my education.*

MARK TWAIN

Brace yourselves: if you go on an information quest, the traditional Hermetic laws or principles are not an easy read, which makes them disconcerting to many a magickal practitioner. Those principles are about as old school as you can get. Considering that they are believed to have been first penned somewhere around 300 BCE, they can be a bit confusing for modern-day practitioners. And, just to make things interesting, there are several modern variations of the Hermetic principles, and they are often arranged in various orders, which makes organized Virgos like me start to get twitchy.

So after several weeks of feeling like I was searching and studying in circles, I finally called a Witch friend for help—okay, actually I shot off several snarky text messages about the problems my research was giving me. Christopher found these so hilarious that he called me later in the day and talked to me while he was driving to go teach a class out of town, thus giving me a booster course on the Hermetic principles over the phone.

He explained that while these principles begin with a broad cosmic base, if you follow them in order, they do become more specific and less lofty, which made me stop banging my head against my reference books long enough to stop and focus.

The seven Hermetic principles form a system that can be studied and applied by anyone willing to put in the time and work. When I added the seven principles to this book, I listed them in the order that two respected Craft teachers teach them to their students.

The seven Hermetic principles *are* a mystery…and, honestly, that is part of their charm. They are not meant to be comprehended in one sitting. Take the time you need to become familiar with them and to allow their information to filter into your own magick.

While researching these principles, I did feel a little overwhelmed at the massive amount of information and the many variations on them. Then I realized that the point was to study them and do my best to integrate their lessons. I had to let the information seep in, and that took time. For folks like me who want to dive in and do something, the frustrating weeks I spent researching did have their own rewards; I had not wasted my time at all. In those reams of notes and stacks of books, I had uncovered something that I least expected.

The turning point for me happened while I was looking yet again at a familiar phrase from the Hermetic principles. I had looked at it dozens of times, but all of a sudden, there it was: to me, it seemed to echo lines from *The Charge of the Goddess*. Now *that* I could wrap my mind around, and I could finally begin to see these Hermetic principles in a whole new light.

The Hermetic principles *are* like building blocks. They support one another, and the first principle is the foundation. I like to picture these principles as stacking up in a seven-stepped pyramid, one principle on top of the next, with each principle supporting the next one; that way, I remember to take them one step at a time. Keep reading and you will see what I mean.

The Seven Hermetic Principles

Rules are not necessarily sacred; principles are.

FRANKLIN D. ROOSEVELT

Here are the seven classic Hermetic principles. I kept them as straightforward as possible, with real-life clarifications where they were applicable and with practical notes at the end. Take your time and let the information settle in; this is not a "I read it once, now I am done" section. Slow down and absorb this, one step at a time. Taking the time to discover and comprehend these Hermetic principles or laws is in itself an act of alchemy whereby you transform both yourself and your prosperity magick, or any other type of magick, into something *more*. The more you know, the stronger and more refined your magick will be.

The Principle of Mentalism

This is the first principle. It states that "all is mind"—that everything exists in the mind of the God/dess, or the divine consciousness. In her book *Power of the Witch*, Laurie Cabot writes of the first principle that "all creation is composed by the Divine Mind." In other words, the Goddess literally *thought* us into being.

To comprehend this principle, you need to realize that we are filled with unlimited potential. Everything that is apparent to our physical, material senses is spirit, and *everything* on the physical and the mental plane is in a process of evolution—which means that we, as Witches, are constantly evolving too. So open up your mind and let the knowledge in. The physical, or mundane, world works by the laws of nature. However, the true nature of power and matter takes a back seat to the mastery of the mind. If your mind is leading the way, then you too can create anything with the power of your mind.

Practical Magick Note: Know that your thoughts can affect your and others' reality. This is vitally important, so remember that thoughts have real substance. Bottom line: thought creates!

The Principle of Correspondence

This principle teaches us that "As above, so below. As within, so without." We do exist on all planes—the astral/spiritual, energetic, and physical—so this principle is a lesson in perspective. When most authors try to explain this "lesson of perspective," often you will read a riff about holograms, which, I confess, makes me lose whatever is left of my mind.

Holograms? *Please.*

One day I was feeling particularly put upon. I was arguing out loud with a reference book's description of holograms and this Hermetic principle of correspondence in particular. I was thinking maybe if I just read it out loud to myself, then I would finally understand the whole hologram explanation thing. Then my husband, who had been quietly and contentedly reading a fly-fishing magazine, looked over at me and said, "Are you talking about dimensions?"

My head snapped up. *Hmmm*…I thought about that. As in a perception of dimensions? Maybe I needed to look inside myself instead of in a stuffy old book…hold on.

Look *within* to learn more.

This was when I connected with a line from *The Charge of the Goddess*: "If that which you seek you find not within yourself, you will never find it without," which is just another way of saying "As within, so without." It is all about how you perceive it. I had to find that answer by looking within before I could find it without—a "light bulb" moment.

Practical Magick Note: The principle of correspondence also directs us to the most harmonious tools and spell accoutrements for our magick, as in a table of correspondences. Specific crystals and herbs can activate certain energies that are naturally associated with your various magickal goals. Color is a prime example. Yellow flowers, especially those with solar shapes like the sunflower, are typically associated or perceived to correspond with the sun, fame, and achievement. The sunflower corresponds with or matches the intention of success. The principle of correspondence is all about perception and association.

The Principle of Vibration

This principle teaches us that all is in motion, nothing is at rest. Everything moves; everything vibrates with its own rate of vibration. Everything is in a constant state of movement and change. Objects, plants, and animals have an energy signature that is often perceived as an aura. Interestingly, when we change our energy or mental state, the world around us changes to match the new vibration.

Now, there are two parts to the principle of vibration. First, there is the law of attraction, often called LOA for short. The LOA shows us that "like attracts like." It proves that what you think—either good or bad—you will attract to yourself. After all, the first principle's lesson was "thought creates"! This is a simple explanation of thoughtforms (and thoughtforms will be discussed in more detail shortly).

Part two of the principle of vibration is the law of change. Witches embrace change, and change is to be expected as normal. Honestly, when we work our magick, are we not working for positive change? It is also important to remember that when we change our conscious behavior or attitude to a more positive one, then the world around us changes as well.

Practical Magick Note: Yes, the principle of vibration is that simple: change your attitude and you change your energetic vibration. That change then ripples out and affects your environment. For example, I always say that the strongest magick comes from the heart, and the heart generates the strongest energetic vibrations. It is magnetic. These heart vibrations are the starting point to all of the positive energies—such as prosperity—that we then can attract into our lives.

The Principle of Polarity

This principle shows us that everything is relative to something else—all things have an opposite, and all things are dual. Poverty is at one end of the scale and wealth is at the other. Also, here is a big mystery for you to wrap your mind around: each of the opposite characteristics contains the essence of the other; the best example of this thought is the yin and yang symbol. There can be poverty in wealth—someone may have every expensive and fancy item that they could dream of, yet they could be miserably alone and poor in true friends—just as there could be wealth in poverty. Someone considered to be living in poverty may feel very fortunate and incredibly blessed simply to be alive and have their family with them.

Opposites do create balance. As Witches, we are walkers between the worlds, searching and exploring the balance between the two extremes at all times. With opposites being identical in nature but different in degrees, it is these subtle shades that we cultivate and work our magick with.

Practical Magick Note: Magick is neither black nor white, good nor evil. The terms "helpful" or "baneful" are simply perceptions of magick's dual nature. Witches work to be neutral—to walk in balance and to work impartially somewhere in the center between the two extremes. This walking neutrally between the worlds is a study in polarity. We are not one or the other but shades of both.

With prosperity magick, the principle of polarity is manifested as giving and receiving. As magick works best through a dynamic energetic exchange, if you happily give then you will abundantly receive. They are two parts of the process, identical in nature but different in degree. Walk in balance, respect polarity, and work with the laws of nature.

The Principle of Rhythm

This principle teaches us that everything flows and all things are in some way circular or cyclical. In order for our magick to be most effective, we must work with the natural rhythms of the seasons, the wheel of the year, the moon, and the rhythm of our lives.

In the spring new life pushes its way into being. Energy, enthusiasm, and new beginnings are the tides of energy. In the summer there is bounty, passion, and growth. The fall brings a time to gather in—to celebrate harvest's bounty and prepare for the fallow time. In the winter we retreat to our warm homes to rest, study, and prepare. All of life exists within an order, or pattern, of cycles. The moon waxes and wanes, the seasons pass one into the other…everything has a cycle and a rhythm. As Witches, we follow those rhythms and ride the wave.

Practical Magick Note: No season is without a rhythm. There is a pulse or cadence—a tempo—to the wheel of the year as it turns. This turning of the wheel has an energetic rhythm of its own. Work with that. Also keep in mind that the principle of rhythm reminds us that for every action there is a reaction, which is sometimes visualized as a pendulum. This is another aspect of rhythm. How we treat others is the way we will be treated in turn. What we send out energetically comes back to us. It's all a manifestation of rhythm.

The Principle of Gender

This principle is simply the law of polarity put in action. Masculine and feminine principles are always at work in the world, whether we recognize them or not. We are all a blending of both masculine and feminine energies.

Classically, feminine energy is considered to be magnetic, as feminine energy draws in and is nurturing and yielding, while masculine energy projects out and is strong and assertive. Imagine how the ideas of magnetic energy and assertive energy can be applied. The possibilities are endless.

> **Practical Magick Note:** The principle of gender works in harmony with creation, and gender manifests on all planes: moon and sun, earth and sky, even in the faces of our goddess and god.

The Principle of Cause and Effect

This principle illustrates that there are no coincidences; nothing happens by chance. Chance is a name for an unrecognized law. I have seen this explained this way: "There are many planes of causation, but nothing escapes the law," which is a classy way to say that for every spell outcome there is a prior action, or cause.

What we send out energetically or through spellwork, be it positive or baneful, will ripple out and return to our own personal world in some way, shape, or form. For every action, there is a reaction. Again, nothing escapes the principle of cause and effect.

> **Practical Magick Note:** By knowing and understanding this final Hermetic principle, we can make more thoughtful choices according to what we want to bring into our life or be rid of. Understanding cause and effect keeps you from feeling like a pawn in the game. You can control

the board and the outcome of your magick when you
work thoughtfully and in awareness of this principle.

• • • • •

Take some time and study the Hermetic principles carefully. While
you are considering the implications of the seven Hermetic principles
for your life and magick, I invite you to take a closer look at the law of
attraction.

The Law of Attraction: It's Not a "Secret"

We dance round in a ring and suppose,
While the secret sits in the middle and knows.

ROBERT FROST

Witches know that *The Secret* isn't a secret at all. It's just a New Agey, popular way to teach the general public a little something about magick and
the power of the principle of vibration and the principle of cause and
effect. The whole message of *The Secret* is that prosperity exists solely
in your mind and it will be drawn to you, which is the down-and-dirty
illustration of the law of attraction at work.

You can manifest your own destiny. The law of attraction works in
all aspects of your life, magickal and mundane, whether you realize it
or not. It enlightens us by showing that our thoughts are actual energy.
Your thoughts do manifest as vibrations, and that vibratory energy ripples out into the universe and becomes real. Thought creates!

So if your inner monologue is always self-defeating, you will attract
defeat straight to you. If your inner monologue is upbeat, then positive
experiences will come your way. You do pull toward yourself whatever
energy you send out into the universe. Working with the law of attraction is an act of applying the Hermetic principles to gain prosperity.

The law of attraction is the law by which thought connects with its object, which makes for the basis of thoughtforms. If you have been studying the Craft for a while, you have probably heard of thoughtforms before. It is interesting to note that thoughtforms are often called the building blocks of magick.

Thoughtforms are created by strong positive thoughts—or intense negative thoughts—that then take on a life of their own and exist on the astral plane. These thoughts on the astral plane can and do manifest and may affect a person's emotional state as well as their spellwork.

Because—say it with me one more time—*thought creates!*

In the most simple of terms: if you believe, then you shall receive. As Witches we use this very sweet, simple idea and combine it with both knowledge and action for successful spellcraft. However, it all does begin with that personal energetic vibration that you radiate. To show you what I mean, consider these four points that fall under the law of attraction:

1: Appreciation and Thankfulness

It is believed that when you think about the things you appreciate—what you are most thankful for and are happy about—this cheerful act raises your energetic vibration. It flares out your aura into a happy, bright color. If you were going to visualize that prosperous color, I would go with gold (for success and healthy abundance) or green (for prosperity and wealth).

Simple fact: appreciating the positive things in your life makes you happy. That happiness builds thoughtforms around you that are vibrant, assured, and successful, which only attracts *more* prosperity and abundance into your world. This is what we call a win-win scenario.

2: Validation and Enthusiasm from the Beginning

Keep track of how the prosperity spells begin to manifest, and celebrate these events as they occur. When you acknowledge your spellwork's manifestations, as in good luck and new opportunities coming your way, this helps to build your enthusiasm. And enthusiasm is contagious!

Building up that positive energy raises your vibratory rate, making it higher and brighter. These positive thoughforms become a brilliant gold or shimmering green. The higher the energy builds, the higher your vibrations. This means that those vibrations become stronger, and they push away doubt. These good vibrations also lessen any resistance to the positive changes that you are casting for.

3: Banish Doubt and Remove Fear of Failure

Doubt is a suffocating word; remove it from your vocabulary, your magick, and your life. If you find yourself thinking, "Gosh, I wonder if this prosperity spell will even work…," you are already halfway to doubt. Bad Witch. No cookie.

This is why in the old days teachers encouraged their students to do a spell and forget about it. While I don't think you should ignore it, you should not smother a spell with worry either. Don't think the process to death, for Goddess's sake. Believe in your magick.

When doubt is removed from your spellcraft, there is no resistance to get in the way of the change. Allow the prosperity work to bloom and grow, and—like water flowing downhill with no resistance—the magick will flow faster. By removing fear of failure, it speeds up your spell's outcome.

If you are starting to let doubt creep in, squash it by thinking and saying something like "My spell is in the process of manifesting and attracting prosperity" or try "My prosperity magick is starting to bloom right now." Be positive. Do not give up.

4: Celebrating and Acknowledging the Outcome

When your prosperity magick has manifested and you are enjoying the outcome, then you should quietly celebrate. Celebrating and acknowledging your spell's success builds even more positive energy for you personally, as these happy, celebratory vibrations will attract even more prosperity to you.

This is the law of attraction, and it will respond to your magickal thoughtforms and the positive energetic vibrations that you send out into the world while you gratefully acknowledge your spell's success. Be cheerful, enjoy your success, and attract more of the same magickal energy into your world! Wrap your mind around the law of attraction and work this into your abundance and prosperity magick for the best results.

Elements of Prosperity Spellwork and Ritual

And harmony means that the relationship
between all the elements used in a
composition is balanced, is good.

KARLHEINZ STOCKHAUSEN

With all the talk of the Hermetic principles and the law of attraction and its guidelines and various points to consider, we need to take a look at the elements of prosperity spellwork and ritual. Why now? Because some folks who are reading this book may be brand-new to spellcasting or need a refresher course. Now, before you cringe and announce that you are too advanced of a practitioner to waste your time reading such material, hang on a second.

The story in the introduction about what made me start to dig deeper into the mechanics of prosperity magick was not put there to fill up space. It was to illustrate that anybody, even a Witch who has three decades under her belt, can make a mistake. We all need to take another look at the basics and strengthen our foundational knowledge from time to time.

No matter who you are, going over the basics or refreshing your information is a smart thing to do. The information and structure from this first chapter will be incorporated into every spell and ritual that you will find in this practical book, so study them carefully and brush up your knowledge and skills.

And so, without further ado:

Purpose and Focus: Be clear with your intention. What is the purpose of the ritual? Are you focused? Did you take a moment to ground and center and to put aside all negativity? Do not focus on fears or wants. Focus on abundance, happiness, positive change, and prosperity. Now ask yourself if your intention is pure. Are you sincere?

The phrase "know thyself" was inscribed on an ancient temple at Delphi. That phrase is an elegant way of reminding you to be balanced and ethical. This is important. You need to be focused and have yourself in a calm, centered state. This is a requirement for altered consciousness. It is easy to forget in the heat of the moment or in the rush to work a quick spell, but do your best to be calm and centered. Take a moment and clear your mind. Find your focus.

Intention and Will: Know your exact intention. Visualize! If you are going to will positive change into your life, then you must have the determination to succeed plus the strength to live your life as a successful, prosperous, and generous person. Focusing your will is a test of your personal strength and of your goal to bring positive change into your world. Thought creates. If you have a positive intention and have focused your will, then directing the energy of the spell will be smooth and effortless.

Raising Personal Vibrations: This flows right after the previous two. Happy, upbeat energetic vibrations build powerful, effective prosperity-attracting thoughtforms. Whatever you are feeling emotionally at the time of the spell will affect the outcome of the magick. Think about the hard lesson I relearned in the introduction. Recall the principle of vibration. Build those positive thoughtforms well and get ready to release them out into the world to effect a positive change.

Sacred Space: Spells and rituals cause a change in consciousness, as they take place outside of ordinary life. Wherever you choose to work your witchery and prosperity magick, make it a sacred space. Set up an attractive and inspiring work surface. By this I mean a clean, happy, pleasant environment, whether you cast in your home or out on your porch, deck, or in the garden. Sacred space is defined as an area that is natural, clean, beautiful, and inspiring.

Supplies: Most rituals employ complementary colored candles, oils, herbs, crystals, and other props. Your supplies should correspond and be harmonious with your intention. Just as was discussed earlier with the principles of correspondence and vibration, the supplies should be in tune with each other, having the same sort of energy and vibration, for best results. (There is a correspondence chart for abundance and prosperity magick included in appendix II, so don't worry about scrambling for a supply list. I've got you covered.)

Timing: It is often remarked that timing is everything, and that is certainly the case with magick. When it comes to magickal timing for your prosperity spells, I am breaking it down into two main categories: the waxing or waning moon and the most favorable days of the week.

> *Waxing Moon:* The waxing moon pulls prosperity in. When the moon is waxing (increasing) in the sky, it's going from new moon to full moon phase. This is the best time for spells that call for increase, expansion, new opportunities, and financial growth.

> *Waning Moon:* The waning moon banishes poverty. When the moon is waning (decreasing) in the sky, it's going from full moon to new moon phase. This is the perfect time for magick that decreases debt, diminishes worry, and removes obstacles to your success. Work *with* the tides of the moon, not against them. Consider the Hermetic principle of rhythm.

> *Specific Days of the Week:* Sometimes we do not have the option of waiting for the correct moon phase. We do, however, have the opportunity to work with astrological energies and daily correspondences. The most opportune days of the week for abundance and prosperity magick are Sunday (the sun's day for success and wealth) and Thursday (Jupiter's day for prosperity and abundance). Consider the principle of correspondence.

Prosperity Is Just Around the Corner:
Are You Ready?

If you want to succeed, you should
strike out on new paths...

JOHN D. ROCKEFELLER

We have begun to travel down an enchanting path with brand-new eyes that allow us to explore and learn about prosperity magick from a fresh and practical perspective. This is a wonderful thing, for when it comes to prosperity magick, you must begin with a positive attitude and be honest about how you view yourself and your place in the world.

Dare to study the mysteries of the seven Hermetic principles. Embrace the law of attraction and reaffirm the elements of spellcraft and ritual. Put this foundational knowledge to good use, and you will find that you are already well on your way to a more prosperous, happy, and abundant life.

This is an exciting time in your journey, as it allows you to see things in your magickal world as if for the first time. So let's turn the page and keep exploring. Up next, we study the element of air and find out how it can propel inspiration, happiness, and abundance into our lives.

Chapter Two

AIR:
HAPPINESS & SUCCESS

*Happiness is a complex path that
becomes easy only as we walk it.*
ANDREA POLARD

THE ELEMENT OF air brings inspiration and creativity into our lives.
In this second chapter we embrace cheerful ideas, attitudes, and brand-
new starts, which will allow some fresh air to billow into our world. By
doing so, we are clearing out those old perceptions and negative attitudes, and we are permitting joy, abundance, and prosperity to thrive.
This is how you put the law of attraction into motion, for once happiness arrives, this encourages enthusiasm and inspiration, allowing for
new magickal perspectives. In the simplest of terms, happiness is the
currency of abundance.

From this point on, you must become aware that the wisdom and
strength that you need to make your dreams come true is already in
your possession. If you have trouble believing that you can actually create an abundant, prosperous future for yourself, then, my witchy friend,
you are allowing your magick to be blocked. Happiness and fulfillment
do not come from external events, and these emotions are not granted
by material things. In reality, happiness and fulfillment are spiritual
matters, and they come from within.

We do have the right to pursue happiness. If that seems a tall order
for you at the moment, I suggest you take a deep breath, relax, and give

yourself a break. You will get there. It is simply time to change your perspective. In life and in magick, it is the simple things that matter the most. If your will and magickal intentions are to create a better outlook, a more upbeat attitude, and a positive prosperous change, then you will do so.

But guess what? That change comes most easily when you allow yourself to take pleasure in your world again and when you permit yourself to be happy. Simple pleasures are often overlooked when it comes to a magickal life. Here is a mystery for you to contemplate: the simpler we make our life, the more abundant we become. You can learn to be happy just as you can learn any new behavior. Make happiness a habit *and* a magickal practice!

The Art of Happiness

Follow your bliss.

JOSEPH CAMPBELL

Embrace what makes you happy! Happiness is not a frivolous extravagance; it is essential to our lives. Do something today that makes you happy—something wonderfully simple. Simple, affordable pleasures are often overlooked. When was the last time you baked some cookies just for fun? Or arranged flowers from your own garden in a vase for inside your home? For that matter, when was the last time you planted some flowers in your garden or tomatoes in containers on your porch? Come on, use your imagination and find something simple that you can do today that will bring you contentment and happiness.

Due to the fast-paced and hectic world we live in today, many of us feel disconnected and tired. We don't enjoy our lives. We just get through and often waste our days wishing that we had a bigger car, that featured house on HGTV, or those really cool designer shoes. We are typically not content with the good things we *do* have. Instead, we yearn for something more extravagant.

I am one of those folks who is not impressed with big houses or fancy cars. Never have been. What personally impresses me are pretty, well-tended gardens; healthy, happy kids; and a long-lasting relationship. Why? Because I know that each of those things takes work—lots of work. Anyone who can pull off any of those feats has had to work at it.

Hard work and the drive to succeed, combined with the ability to be happy, is impressive, and it's worth admiring. Remember that it is not about the things. It is, in fact, about the quality of your life and what you do with it that makes for a prosperous and abundant existence.

So, live on the edge and do something that brings you joy. Have a cup of tea in front of a roaring fire. Share a bottle of wine with your love while sitting under a tree. Take the kids to the park, pick out a nice spot in the shade, and let them run around on the playground and scream like maniacs for a while…or join them. Go on, it's fun to run around with your kids. As long as you are at the playground, find a swing and see how high you can go. There is something so freeing about swinging up in the air. You can always take a walk at sunrise (or sunset) or meet a friend for coffee. It is the simple things in life that make us feel the most content.

Learn to savor life's satisfying little moments. For example, spending a few quiet, productive hours in a study room at the local library, working on this manuscript, made me pretty darn happy. Sometimes a change of perspective is called for—in my case, getting out of the house and doing something different with my writing routine.

You may be wondering what all these simple suggestions for happiness have to do with your own personal prosperity. Well, we need to get that law of attraction mojo working for you. We also need to settle you firmly in a positive mood and break the pattern of any lingering negative and worrisome thoughts. Here is where we snap you out of any old ideas or patterns of negative thinking. This action is called a "pattern interrupt."

Changing your perspective and doing something different is a positive thing. It forces you to stop, look around, and consider exactly where you are standing at this moment of your life. A pattern interrupt causes you to shift your perceptions—and it works just like magick.

Pattern Interrupt

And now for something completely different…

MONTY PYTHON

You *can* change negative and unwanted thought patterns. All it takes is some will and intention on your part. As Witches, we already should be very familiar with focusing our will and our intentions. So we have an edge, and this technique comes pretty easily to us.

Pattern interrupt was originally a hypnotherapy technique. It is designed to shift your focus and, best of all, to neutralize negative thinking. Whenever you feel frustrated or worried, you can successfully use a pattern interrupt technique. It will knock you out of that feeling of being stuck.

When we are in a negative pattern in our lives, we tend to go over and over self-defeating thoughts. It's a vicious cycle. The more we worry, the more depressed we feel. The more down we feel, the more we worry…. That old inner monologue may go a little something like this: "I am so worried about money…nothing works; no matter what spell I try, I'll never get out of this mess. It doesn't matter what I do, the magick always flops anyway…"

Oh boy. Think about what sort of energy those negative thoughts are creating in the physical world. Remember thoughtforms? All that negativity is creating something, and it (the negative thoughtforms) will keep following you around, looking for more energy to feed on, making you feel worse and dragging you down.

We now know from the Hermetic principles that "thought creates." So it is vitally important to stop that destructive cycle. You need to recognize that those negative thoughts and patterns of defeatist behavior are getting in your own magickal way. So now that you have identified the problem, it's time to interrupt that old cycle.

Instead of worrying about all those negatives and building more negative energy, consider what you would like to have happen instead.

When you catch yourself in those pessimistic thought patterns, stop. Take a breath and make the effort to change your attitude and your energy.

Come on, you are a magickal practitioner! Suck it up and make a change. Use your will and your intention, and put some effort into it. Take a deep breath, call upon the element of air to blow away any hovering negativity, and create a positive change. Now shift your energetic focus. Transform that inner monologue into something positive and constructive. Try something simple, like this: "As of today, I am changing my perception and attitude about abundance and prosperity. Abundance and prosperity is all around me. This new, positive energy is now flowing into my life. As I will it, so shall it be!"

Then do something completely different. Employ a pattern interrupt. Change your environment and your surroundings (thus interrupting your pattern of behavior to support your shift in the pattern of your thoughts). This is deceptively simple, but it works surprisingly well. For example, if you typically work out first thing in the morning, change that. Try working out after your shift ends at your job or work out in the evenings for a while. Shake up your routine. It will kick your brain into a whole new way of thinking and it forces you to adjust your attitude.

Here are a few more suggestions. If you eat lunch at your desk at work, then go outside, sit on the grass, and eat lunch in the sunshine. Use the affirmation from above. As you will it, then so shall it be.

Now, if you work at home and feel stifled and closed in, then load up your notes and laptop and sit outside on the back porch or in the garden—or get out of the house altogether.

I am very grateful to be able to work at home, and I love it here in my little office, but sometimes I do feel the walls closing in. On average I put in eight- to ten-hour days in my home office, and I rarely take a day off from writing. I love a routine and work better with one. However, everyone (even me) needs to shake up their daily routine and do something different once in a while.

I have several writer friends who, when they need a change of scenery, set up at a booth in the local coffee shop, and they swear by it. They happily pound away on their laptops, slurp fancy coffee, and write away. While I love the scents of a coffee shop, I personally can't work in all that noise. The loud conversations and the clanging of the cutlery is jarring to me, sort of like nails on a chalkboard. But I have given it the old college try. Also, I don't drink coffee. I know, I know, it's like sacrilege to be a writer who hates coffee. I like the smell of it, though, so that has to count for something…

Anyway, when I need to break out of my rut or if a chapter runs away from me, occasionally I will get out of the house and get a bowl of soup, a smoothie, or a cup of lowfat hot chocolate. I will sit in a local coffee shop and enjoy the hustle and bustle as an observer. I people-watch and think deep thoughts and enjoy myself for a little while. Then, when the noise gets to be too much, I head to the library to get some work done.

With my laptop, reference books, and notes in tow, I rent a study room for a few hours. The change of pace from the noise and action of the coffee shop to the different and quiet surroundings of the library jolts me out of any mental blocks or frustration (and yes, this would be a pattern interrupt). It is an action that gets me out of the house and gives me a change of scenery. I get a lot of work done at the library. I save the "work at the library days" for when I really need them. It is a way to take a negative, frustrated mood and turn it into something positive, constructive, and enjoyable.

Another nifty pattern interrupt trick I recently discovered is to change the playlist on my iPod. We all have our favorite tunes, and technology has allowed us all to create a personal soundtrack to our lives. Shake yours up a bit and add some new music or some old favorites to that soundtrack. Music aligns to the element of air, after all.

While working on this air-themed chapter, I made a whole new eclectic playlist and entitled it "Happiness and Creativity." I loaded up some '70s and '80s music, tunes from Broadway shows such as *The Addams Family Musical*, and some fun current hits that make me smile while I sing along. It's a wild mix but it makes me happy, it changes my mood, and it works amazingly well.

You have the power to change your life—to experience abundance, happiness, and fulfillment—and it starts right now. Be willing to shift your perceptions. Interrupt any patterns of negative behavior and thoughts. Act as you desire to be.

Reclaim your happiness and your personal power. Express your talents fully and live as you choose. Practice keeping your mind peaceful and centered. Employ a pattern interrupt if you need to, and really work on becoming a happier person. You will find that success is more easily obtained when you do.

A Floral Fascination to Reinforce a Positive Attitude

You have the power to change your life and enjoy happiness, success, and abundance. That power is right at your witchy fingertips. This simple and cheerful spell will help you to reinforce a positive attitude, and it can be performed at any time. A "floral fascination" is a phrase I coined several years ago. It means a straightforward spell or charm worked only with flowers that can be used for various magickal purposes. Do not underestimate the power of floral fascinations; they work very well indeed. The great thing about this type of spellwork is that it is subtle. You could easily take a floral fascination along with you to work. A flower in a vase on your desk is very subtle, enjoyable magick.

The supplies are simple and may be purchased inexpensively or gathered from your own gardens. You will need a yellow flower for the element of air and for cheerfulness and success.

A bright yellow rose increases positive emotions. A spicy yellow carnation brings cheerful energy and boosts your mood. If you have yellow flowers blooming in your garden at the moment, use those. Consider coreopsis, ornamental sunflowers, daylilies, daisies, or mums. Any of those sunshine-colored flowers would add the right positive mood and magick to your floral fascination.

Slip the flower or flowers into a vase filled with fresh water and center the vase in a spot where you will see it and enjoy it every day. On your desk at work, your dresser in the bedroom, or the table in the kitchen—wherever you feel it should go. Hold your hands out over the blossoms and say the following charm three times:

By blossom and color this spell is begun
My attitude is now a positive one.
By the element of air, this floral spell is cast
The energy breezes around and goes to work fast.
Happiness and cheer now come to me
And as I will it, so shall it be.

Enjoy the flower until it starts to fade, then neatly return it to nature by adding it to a compost pile or to your yard waste to be recycled. Wash the vase and save it for another bouquet.

Blessed be.

Happiness and Success

Success is not the key to happiness.
Happiness is the key to success.

HERMAN CAIN

As I continued to research the topic of abundance and success, I kept running into the idea of "authentic happiness." Would you even recognize authentic happiness if it came up and hugged you? Think about it. Authentic happiness would be some of your best, happiest times and fondest memories.

A few years ago I did an East Coast tour for *Garden Witch's Herbal* in early June. I planned, set up, and paid for the trip myself. I had booked five author events in three states over an eight-day period of time. Honestly, it was much more expensive than I had planned on, which I did not discover until we were on the road and about three days into the tour. (Well, you have to learn these things somehow…) After the first two events, reality set in. I realized I had seriously underestimated our expenses, and I began to worry about the mounting cost of the tour.

I had never taken my husband on tour with me before, but we were determined to enjoy the trip no matter what. I soon realized that my fretting over the cost of our travel was squashing any sense of fun that we might have on the trip. After my author events finished up in Maine, my husband and I decided to use our travel day as a sort of day off and check out a Victorian-era botanical garden in New Hampshire. The fastest way to cheer me up is to take me to a garden, after all. So, armed with a GPS and a New Hampshire tourism brochure, we set out.

The garden was small but absolutely enchanting, and we did have fun exploring and taking lots of pictures. According to the local map we picked up, we were very near the ocean, so we asked a volunteer at the botanical garden how close we actually were. Her directions were simple: turn right out of the parking lot, follow the road, and look to your left.

We finished up our tour and decided to explore. We followed the road as directed, and, to our amazement, realized that we were indeed right along the shore. Actually, we were in the Hamptons, which we found hilarious. A couple of average Midwesterners from the 'burbs cruising along in the Hamptons. So we drove along, gaping at the massive homes along the ocean, and then we discovered a public beach. Parking was about two dollars an hour, and we happily paid the meter and raced each other to the ocean. It was warm and sunny that day, but the water was freezing cold—which explained the lack of beach-goers. We basically had that public beach all to ourselves. Perfect.

There was an adorable little food place across the road from the beach, and we decided to stay put and get lunch right there. For seating there were about a half-dozen wooden tables with umbrellas under the shade of some pine trees. For lunch we chose lobster rolls. It was forty bucks for two sandwiches served on paper plates. I could only sputter at the total, but my husband just looked at me and told me to take a deep breath and relax.

He asked me quietly, when would we ever be here again in the Hamptons, eating fresh lobster rolls and looking at the ocean? Point taken. It made me think of that clever commercial: Parking meter at beach, two dollars per hour. Lobster rolls for lunch, forty dollars. Memories of unplanned day on beach with husband? Priceless.

Spending time on the Hamptons beach had not been part of our travel plans, but I reminded myself as I doled out the cash for the lobster rolls that this was an adventure, and one is not supposed to plan an adventure. (Even though as a Virgo I probably would still give it my best shot.) My husband just grinned at me happily and we sat at an old wooden picnic table in the shade and looked at the ocean and ate lunch. The food was phenomenal, the atmosphere was relaxing, and the view was amazing.

Later in the day we found a hotel for the night about five miles in from the beach. We drove through a little town and discovered a grocery store and a couple of fast-food restaurants. We checked into the hotel, dumped our stuff, and headed back to the beach.

Because we had blown our food budget for the day on those lobster rolls, we ended up going to a McDonald's for dinner. We rolled out of the drive-thru and then drove straight back to the beach, laughing the whole way.

So there we were, eating our dinner from the fast food dollar menu on the Hamptons beach. *Tres chic!* We finished our dinner, threw away the trash, and walked through the surf, picking up stones and shells, until sunset.

We took a few selfies with the digital camera that evening—you know, where you hold your arm way out to take your own picture. Well, it must have been the thrill of the cheap fast food in the Hamptons, because one of the pictures turned out so great that we had it blown up and framed when we got home.

Here is the funny thing…to this day, that unplanned afternoon on the beach in the Hamptons is one of my fondest memories. My husband and I got beach time in a beautiful and relaxing spot, we ate hideously expensive lobster rolls for lunch, and then we finished our day by eating extremely cheap fast food in one of the ritziest places in the United States, which really appeals to my sense of humor.

Dollar-menu hamburgers on the beach in the Hamptons was definitely a moment of authentic happiness for us, or I suppose if you want to get technical it was an authentic *day* of happiness. That afternoon turned my overall view of the trip around, and I was able to enjoy the rest of the time on the East Coast and finish a successful book tour. Attitude is everything.

New Mindset, New Attitude

You are the embodiment of the information
you choose to accept and act upon. To change
your circumstances, you need to change
your thinking and subsequent actions.

ADLIN SINCLAIR

Happiness and optimism can become a learned behavior. Put thoughts of lack behind you and become optimistic. Oh, and really try to stop worrying; it is a terrible waste of energy, after all. We can change our attitude and our outlook if we are willing to put some work into it.

May I point to those Hermetic principles from chapter 1? The very first principle shows us that thought creates! So ask yourself, what is all of that worry and negativity really bringing into your world? Answer: it is generating self-destructive and negative thoughtforms.

So come to terms with this and regroup. Now you understand why you need to stop this behavior right away. To be honest, the very idea of self-created negative thoughtforms sends some magickal folks into a panic. I don't want you to panic; what I want is for you to be aware. Breathe. Focus and concentrate. Think about it this way: if you created these negative thoughtforms (accidentally or not), then you can certainly get rid of them.

I am not saying that it won't be hard to change your attitude, but do it anyway. Banish those old, gloomy thoughtforms with a smile. You have moved past that now, and you no longer need to have them following you about like funky gray storm clouds. You must lift your awareness above and beyond fear and lack. The subconscious mind accepts whatever we choose to believe. It is important to recognize that sometimes gloomy thoughts can get in the way of our success. So we are going to get rid of those thoughtforms because we do not want any lingering depressive energy hampering the success of our future prosperity magick.

We all need an attitude adjustment from time to time. We have to learn to focus on the positive and change our mindset into something more open and constructive. The ability to honestly and quietly reflect on your life is one of the most powerful tools for personal growth. Just don't dwell on it—instead, think of it as a learning experience, for now that you have evaluated the past, you can envision a bright and open future. Everything we think is, in fact, creating our future. Knowledge and information is power, so put it to good use.

Consider the information presented in this chapter, and get to work. Employ a pattern interrupt, shake up your routine, and look at things differently. It will give you a fresh perspective and encourage a new mindset.

If you will the changes into your life with magickal intention, they will happen. State your intention to change your attitude. Go ahead and visualize any negativity or ill-tempered thoughtforms blowing away and breaking apart like storm clouds being blown apart and dissipated by the wind. Visualize the change to your life that you want and know deep down that it is possible. Now move happily forward in your life as you wish to be.

Wind Chime Magick to
Break Up Negative Thoughtforms

Here is a wind chime spell that employs the element of air and the magick of sound to break up any negative thoughtforms that may stand in the way of your success and prosperity. Choose a set of new wind chimes with a design and sound that appeals to you. Then every time you hear the chimes ring out on a breeze, imagine that their music is breaking up old worries and pessimistic thoughtforms.

To begin the spell, hang up a bewitching set of wind chimes on your porch. Hold your hands on the chimes and enchant them for magickal purpose with this charm, repeating the main spell verse three times:

> With my will and intention this spell is begun
> By the element of air, this magick is spun.
> As of this moment, these wind chimes are now enchanted
> By the winds that do blow, may my success be granted.
> Negative thoughtforms will break apart at the sounds of these chimes
> Happiness, optimism, and success will surely be mine.

Give the wind chimes a little push so they ring out, then close the spell with these final four lines:

> Now sweetly chime and ring out with your happy sound
> No more negativity will ever be found.
> By the element of air, this simple spell was cast
> Let the energy ripple out and the magick last.

Good Mood, Good Magick:
Wow, This Stuff Really Works!

It's kind of fun to do the impossible.

WALT DISNEY

While I researched and wrote this book, I experimented with various magickal spells and charms of my own. However, this time I worked very thoughtfully, using my research. I made sure that I kept those foundational principles in mind, and I also worked on maintaining a positive outlook and a happier attitude. I built positive thoughtforms, and I embraced gratitude while casting prosperity and good luck spells for myself and my family.

The results were pretty impressive. My husband got a pay raise when we really needed one. Then my daughter got a promotion and a pay raise at her job. I knew I was on a roll when an acquaintance called to tell me that she had four free tickets to *The Addams Family Musical* that she could not use. She wondered if I would like to have them. I could only squeal in excitement. I had wanted to see that show so badly, but the tickets for the national tour were way out of my price range. These tickets even came with a parking pass and were VIP club seats at the Fox Theater in St. Louis!

Giddily, I drove an hour to meet her and pick up those tickets. To say thank you, I gave her a nice bottle of wine wrapped up and tucked in a cute Halloween metal bucket. I ended up taking my husband, daughter, and a visiting friend from out of town to the musical. We all had a blast at the show.

After that, my sons dropped by for a visit and then requested that I cast some good luck magick for them. So with a firm grasp on the Hermetic principles and a happy attitude in place, I started working for them as well. A week later, my oldest son called me and was very excited. He'd had a customer walk up to him at his job at a local store where he is a department manager and hand him two baseball playoff tickets—right out of the blue.

This gentleman was a regular at the store. He had walked up to my son while he was stocking shelves and said hello. When Kraig stopped to talk to him, the older gentleman asked him what he would be doing that night, to which my son responded that he and his brother would be watching the Cardinals playoff game at their apartment.

The man smiled and suggested that Kraig take his brother to the playoff game instead. He handed him two tickets and told him to have a good time. Shocked, my son asked him what he wanted for the tickets, as trying to get tickets to the final playoff games was impossible, not to mention very expensive. The gentleman only smiled and told him they were a gift. He just wanted to give them to someone who would truly enjoy them. Amazed, my son thanked him, and the customer left with a wave and a chuckle.

The boys called to tell me the news on their way down to the stadium. The playoff tickets were bleacher seats, close to the field and in a prime location. They were so excited to be going to that game. It ended up that the game my sons went to was the final playoff game—when the Cardinals won and clinched their trip to the World Series. How cool is that?

Blessings and Gratitude

Gratitude is an opener of locked-up blessings.

MARIANNE WILLIAMSON

Gratitude is a skill that we must learn and master in our lifetime. To be grateful is a part of the magick (some would say mystery) when it comes to attracting prosperity, abundance, and happiness into your life.

Gratitude may be understood as a feeling of thankfulness, appreciation, and gratefulness. Stop for a moment and truly consider how rich you are. You are living and breathing. You are able to study as you choose and pursue your religious freedom. You have friends, family, pets, loved ones…the list can go on and on. Reevaluate and realize that you are very rich indeed. This is what makes you feel blessed. Gratitude in itself can become a spiritual practice, for when you focus on the blessings in your life you do change your vibrational rate. This act then attracts even more happiness and abundance into your world. Again, as we discussed in the first chapter, this is an example of the law of attraction at work. Those more optimistic thoughts do breed positive, energetic thoughtforms, and these will then help to create a more upbeat and prosperous reality.

When you are grateful, you are allowing—you are permitting more happiness and abundance to manifest into your world. Your mood is now optimistic because you are behaving and thinking in a more positive frame of mind. There is no time for uncertainty or dissatisfaction, not with all of this happy energy swirling around your life.

So you betcha your abundance magick and prosperity spells will work! It all depends on what energy you embrace. Happiness is contagious and it changes everything. Be willing to let old ideas and negative thoughtforms blow right out of your life. Allow happiness and abundance to breeze in and change your world.

Embrace the blessings you have and become open to receiving even more. Your personal energy will become higher and brighter. In other words, you are putting the blessed in the "blessed be"!

Go, you! Being happy is a great magickal boost. When you are willing to believe in the wonder of magick again, just about anything is possible.

Chapter Three

FIRE:
ILLUMINATION,
TRANSFORMATION &
MANIFESTATION

To move ahead you need to believe in
yourself…have conviction in your beliefs and
the confidence to execute those beliefs.

ADLIN SINCLAIR

THE ELEMENT OF fire is the driving force behind magick. Fire is a spiritually creative natural element that has a life all its own. This element may be loving, but it can also be cruel. Fire's energy is actively passionate in that it is creative and destructive at the same time.

Think of it this way: for something new to flourish, then something old and unneeded must decline and give way. We want to transform those old bad vibes and that sour outlook or any negativity and frustrations that may be hindering your prosperity into something better and more energetically correct.

The element of fire allows new, positive things to emerge into your magickal life right out of the ashes of what no longer serves you. Fire creates illumination and motivation—the motivation that you will need to change and transform your life. And in order to transform and make a difference in your magickal life, you must be different and react differently.

49

Transformation is an important goal for any Witch or magician to focus upon. However, you need to remember that the spells you will be performing are *not* all about money. Money itself does not have the ability to bring prosperity. Many people allow the idea of money to have a sort of power over them. In truth, we do not control money, for money is a commodity.

It is also important not to confuse money with prosperity, though it does have an energetic essence that we can and will tap in to. Consider this: to be prosperous is to be growing, blossoming, or flourishing. In other words, to be prosperous is to be successful. What you want to see manifesting with your magick is change, movement, expansion, and transformation.

Prosperity is a tool that can help to transform your life in meaningful ways so you can thrive on a spiritual level as well as a monetary one. Prosperity is simply the means by which we can smooth the progress of your life's true purpose. You will have to work to achieve your goals; there is no such thing as a free lunch when magick is involved. But if you are willing to get motivated and work hard, you will certainly enjoy the fruits of a magickal and energetic transformation.

To begin this energetic transformation, you need to be true to yourself. Be happy and work on your self-confidence. This is why the Hermetic principles and the foundations of good magick were at the beginning of this book, followed by suggestions on how to embrace happiness and success: there is a spiritual plan in place here. In actuality, we are working our way forward, page by page, to a more prosperous life, as every magickal step we take builds on the previous chapter's lessons and information.

This type of magickal awareness is crucial, as it brings clarification to your goals. Here is an illuminating thought: you are the source of your own prosperity. Remember the discussion of thoughtforms from the previous chapter? Your thoughts do have substance—as in the first Hermetic principle: thought creates! In a very real way, those thoughts set up the model of what is to be created. Your emotions energize the thoughts and propel them from the mental realm into the physical one, thus bringing about the manifestation of your spellwork. The more motivated you become, the stronger and more positive your emotions and the quicker you can transform your life.

Avoid Conflicting Spiritual Energies:
Be Careful What You Cast For

Success is simple. Do what's right,
the right way, at the right time.

ARNOLD H. GLASGOW

As you begin to work your magick for prosperity and abundance, keep your mind focused on your magickal intention and keep your thoughts positive. This way you avoid derailing your spell with any conflicting energies. Whatever we are feeling and thinking during our prosperity spellwork, we will attract into our magick. Case in point: my story in the introduction. If you focus on your fears and gloomy thoughts such as poverty, stress, and worries over looming bills or a lack of cash, you will pull exactly that type of unhelpful energy into your life with your spell. That energy will manifest in unexpected and unwanted ways in your magick, so think carefully before you begin casting.

Many times, people will cast blindly for cash (without being very specific). Perhaps they toss out a spell for, let's say, five thousand dollars, and maybe their magick worked just dandy. The only problem is that their beloved grandfather had to die and leave the money to them as part of an inheritance.

Never cast for abundance without being specific. Perhaps you cast for an abundant garden and a wealth of plant growth…and suddenly you have an abundance of poison ivy taking over. *Be very clear and specific when you cast for prosperity and abundance.* Whether you want to avoid the old lottery curse or an unfortunate situation or an overabundance of something unhealthy or annoying, such as an abundance of stomach flu in your family or that pesky poison ivy in your magickal garden. Stop. Think. Be specific.

Here is another classic example: if you are working a prosperity spell to find a new and better-paying job, do *not* get yourself all in a twist about how much you hate your current job. That is conflicting spiritual energy. Seriously, do you imagine that any spell cast is going to manifest the way you want it to if you are all wound up and pissed off about your current job?

Ah, the answer would be no.

Here is something else I want you to keep in mind. There is this little thing I call the "I hate this job!" backfire. This occurs when you are so wound up and angry about the state of your current job that you cast a spell to get out of the job quickly so you can find a new one. And guess what happens? Typically you get handed your walking papers within a matter of days because you were not specific enough in your request, and the energies that you unleashed in anger and frustration manifested just as you asked. Ta-da! And now you no longer have a job.

The universe has just provided you with lots of time to focus on finding a new one. You wanted out of this job quickly? You got it. This is a classic example of conflicting spiritual energies, with no one to blame but yourself for not thinking it through, not remembering the principles magick is founded upon, and not putting a thoughtful, magickal plan of action into place. So, take this opportunity to go over those Hermetic principles again and make sure you have a firm grasp on them before your next work-related spell.

Also, bear in mind that when you are working any magick in a job environment that may potentially affect many people, you need to be extremely cautious. You want a raise? You want the boss to notice your hard work? Great! Now consider all of the options magick-wise. A spell that manifests with someone else losing their position so that you can take it is poor magick indeed. You want to make yourself and your own hard work shine, not make someone else fail.

You know the old Craft adage about how a spell is like tossing a pebble into a pond? Well, not only does the energy from the splash caused by the tossed pebble ripple out across the water, that pebble now also affects the bottom of the pond and the environment of that pond forever. So if you start carelessly tossing spells around the workplace, you can affect many other people. Poorly planned magick cast at your current job often causes a ripple effect and it can manifest into blocks to your magickal goals. That magick may cause office dramas, delays to your progress, and lots of emotional "pebbles" to pick up at work.

Only cast on yourself in a work environment. Be upbeat and positive when you work your magick. Include a tagline that ensures no one else is adversely affected when your spell unfolds. Try the following tagline for those workplace scenarios:

> I *now cast this spell for just myself; no one else will be affected.*
> *With harm to none, my prosperity spell goes only as directed.*

Again, a "tagline" is literally spoken at the end of a spell—sort of like an insurance policy for the magickally minded. This specific tagline will help keep any workplace magick on task and directed toward your personal, specific goal.

Being Optimistic with Your Prosperity Spells

Change your thoughts and you change your world.

NORMAN VINCENT PEALE

Please remember that it is better to have bright, cheerful, radiant energy than gloom and despair all around you as you cast prosperity spells. Be sure that your mood is upbeat, or at the very least businesslike and neutral. Turn your thoughts to the happy things in your life (whatever they may be) and let this positive energy fill you up. This shift to a more optimistic mood will help your prosperity magick to manifest in positive and more constructive ways. Find and focus on something that you can be grateful for as you work your prosperity magick.

I am going to repeat myself here: *When you are grateful, you are allowing more happiness and abundance to manifest into your world. Your mood is now optimistic because you are behaving and thinking in a more positive frame of mind.*

So allow those positive thoughtforms to build into a more successful you. This way your spells will have a greater level of success.

It is vitally important to realize that your emotions combined with your words infuse your thoughts with a deeper energetic vibration. We are aware that thought does create, so take it a step further and imagine what sort of punch the magickally spoken word packs.

Rhyme, Rhythm, and Repetition:
The Three Rs of the Spell Verse

No, I was not born under a rhyming planet.

WILLIAM SHAKESPEARE

There is a very good reason why most spell verses and charms are written in rhyming couplets. And no, it is not because the writer has delusions of grandeur or wants to be the next Shakespeare. Spell verses typically rhyme so the vocal energy that they create radiates out in a smooth motion. If you want to get technical, sound is a regular mechanical vibration that travels through matter.

When a spell verse or charm is spoken aloud with intention, the energy it creates brings to life a magickal transformation. The sound of your voice combined with your intention ripples out onto the astral plane and then eventually manifests on the physical plane.

Spell verses that rhyme have a beat, not unlike the beat of music. That there is a rhythm or a beat to life is an elemental truth, both in our own bodies (our heartbeats) and in the cycles of nature that surround us. Think of the principle of rhythm, which teaches us that everything flows and that all things are cyclical. This makes the practice of rhythm very important in spells.

If you have ever been to a big Pagan festival and listened to the drummers, the sound is hypnotic. And if you ever watch the drummers, they always seem to be in their own little world. Rhythm puts you in a sort of spell, or trance if you like, because rhythmic sounds change the stream of consciousness. The rhythm and rhyme of spell verses actually ease you into an altered state of consciousness, which is called the alpha state.

Alpha is a state of consciousness that is associated with relaxation, meditating, and peaceful wakefulness. When you enter an alpha state, your mind is alert, clear, and receptive to information on many levels. During the alpha state, you are also open to extrasensory types of communication such as clairvoyance, precognition, and clairaudience. Your intuition turns on and you can feel or see that the magick is working. In her book *Power of the Witch*, Laurie Cabot says of alpha that it "is the springboard for all psychic and magical workings. It is the heart of Witchcraft."

By speaking charms that rhyme and have rhythm, you actually help yourself into that tranquil state of alertness. While you are in the alpha state, your brain is focused and aware, and your inner magick is stimulated. As to why many charms and spell verses call for repetition, the answer is beautifully simple. The more times the spell verse is repeated, the farther into alpha you go. Usually spells call for a triple repetition, which helps explain the classic tagline added to many a spell and charm:

> *By all the power of three times three*
> *As I will it, then so shall it be.*

Not only does the spell verse rhyme, it also has nine syllables per line. There is a meter and rhythm. Also, nine is the outcome of three times three. Mystery solved as to why I have included this tagline in so many of the spells and charms I have written in my books over the years.

Candle Magick:
Tapping into the Fire of Transformation

Candle burning unites our spirit
with the candle's flame.

ILEANA ABREV

Why is candle magick so darn popular? Well, for several reasons. To begin with, it is a direct link to the element of fire. Candle magick is simple, easy, and—bottom line—it gets results. In reality, a burning spell candle is like a signal to the Divine. It sends a message out to the astral realm that magick is afoot and spells are at work. The flame of the spell candle radiates light and transformative energy into the universe. It also symbolizes the spellcaster's intent.

As a whole, people both magickal and mundane respond to candlelight in positive and miraculous ways. The light of candles helps distance us from the hectic and stressful outside world and guides us softly into the beautiful realm of magick.

Candles that are burned with a specific goal in mind become powerful magickal tools. In truth, that little spell candle you are contemplating using right now is a symbol in and of itself. Primal in meaning and a powerful instrument of elemental magick, a lit candle naturally brings illumination and corresponds to the element of fire and the magick of transformation. When spell candles are inscribed with a magickal symbol and then blessed, they really pack a punch.

Spell Candles and Symbolism

Symbols are the imaginative signposts of life.

MARGOT ASQUITH

Symbolism is an important aspect in spellwork, and it should be utilized here. Symbolism is defined as the use of symbols to represent things such as ideas or emotions. Symbolism may be complex or it can be beautifully simple. The practice of symbolism is central to all religions, and we as Witches and magicians often attach favored symbols to our magickal intent according to the situation and our specific need. We do this instinctively, as those symbols give our minds something to work with. In a real way they grant us steppingstones between our wishes and dreams and the physical manifestation of our magick.

Inscribing a spell candle with symbols aligned to prosperity and abundance is a way to program the candle for a specific purpose. The physical tool used for inscription will vary from practitioner to practitioner. Some Witches prefer to use a straight pin, a toothpick, or the tip of a kitchen knife to engrave or to inscribe their spell candles. Personally, I use a boline, which is a knife that has a curved, sickle-shaped blade. (The blade looks like a crescent moon.) The boline is the knife that I use to harvest my magickal herbs, and it is sharp, so I always slow down and take my time when I use it. I have a coven sister who only uses a specific crystal point to carve symbols into her spell candles. It is all about personal preference.

For our purposes here, the prosperity spell candle could be engraved with a corresponding symbol such as a cornucopia, dollar sign, pentagram, crescent moon, or the rune Fehu (ᚠ), which symbolizes victory, wealth, and prosperity. Or you could try the astrological symbol for the planet Jupiter (♃) or for the sun (☉).

Sometimes you can simply engrave words or short phrases on the side of the candle: *good luck at my interview* or *a better, new job.* You could even try *a job that will meet my needs and make me happy.* (Granted, you would need a larger pillar type of candle for that last verse.) But think about it and come up with a positive and specific statement.

Once you have a symbol or phrase in mind—and before you start carving away—then you may move on to the next step in the process:

Enchanting Your Spell Candles

Magic is believing in yourself; if you can do
that, you can make anything happen.

JOHANN WOLFGANG VON GOETHE

The act of enchanting or blessing a candle for your magickal workings is the next step in your candle magick routine. To enchant literally means "to sing to." To enchant something means that you load, or charge, the object with your personal power and positive intentions. This "enchanting" segment is a two-part process, as first you send energy into the candle when you enchant it, and then that programmed energy is released as the spell candle burns.

To begin enchanting your prosperity spell candles, take the unlit spell candle in your hands and focus on it. If you are going to inscribe it, now is the moment. Keep your thoughts calm and on the task at hand as you inscribe or engrave your spell candles.

Next, you will need to visualize your prosperity goals. As thought creates and our magick is affected by our moods, be sure to shift your energetic signature to a correct one. By being in a positive state, this will help your prosperity magick to manifest in affirmative and more constructive ways.

Yes, I am harping on this "positive and happy mood" part. It is important, as it can make the difference between a spell that smoothly manifests and one that just bursts out and causes more problems.

Here is an all-purpose blessing for your spell candles. Hold the inscribed candle in your hands and repeat the verse three times:

All-Purpose Blessing for a Spell Candle

As I hold this magickal spell candle in my hands
I empower it to send magick across the land.
Now burn with purpose, both bright and true
May I be blessed in all that I do.

Once you are done enchanting the candle, you may continue with your spellwork as is your regular routine.

Thinking Outside the Crayon Box:
Candle Colors for Prosperity Magick

Colors, like features, follow the
changes of the emotions.

PABLO PICASSO

Color magick is associated with the element of fire. Technically, color derives from the spectrum of light interacting with the eye's sensitivity to light receptors. Color has a life and energy all of its own. We do know that color affects mood, emotions, and even behavior. It is a powerful tool to employ for transformation.

Most folks assume that the only color for prosperity magick is green. After all, green is the color of currency and the earth, of life and growth. There are a few Witches out there who stretch their thinking further and logically work with metallic gold colors in their abundance and prosperity spells, as this color corresponds with the sun and success. But wait…there's more! There is a whole rainbow of colors out there that you can successfully employ in prosperity magick. It's time to think outside of the crayon box.

For example, royal blue is associated with the planet Jupiter, as are the colors of purple and green. Jupiter is linked to prosperity, which means that royal blue and purple would both also be harmonious to your prosperity spells. This links to the Hermetic principle of correspondence.

Magick has survived for so long because wise folks knew how to improvise and adapt. They worked with what they had on hand or could find or make themselves. Choosing a specific color in your prosperity magick will help you fine-tune your magick.

Candle Colors for Prosperity Magick

Black: removes obstacles and negativity

Gold: wealth, fortune, riches, success

Green: beginning, fertility, the classic prosperity/abundance magick color

Orange: energy, anti-depressive, enthusiasm, harvest, abundance

Pale Green: growth, new projects

Pink: growth, fertility, self-love, contentment

Purple: power, psychic ability, a Jupiter color

Red: strength, courage, determination, helps remove blocks

Royal Blue: flow, inspiration, a Jupiter color

Silver: astral energies, goddess magick, finances

White: an all-purpose candle color

Yellow: the sun's color, emotional health, success, winning

Two Candle Spells for Success and Prosperity

*Why is it that every time I am with
you makes me believe in magic?*

ROBERT A. HEINLEIN

Here are a duo of candle spells for you to work that will help you in your prosperity goals. The first uses a green seven-day jar candle, and the second a bright blue votive candle.

Green Jar Candle Spell

Timing: For best results, work this spell during a waxing moon phase. Corresponding days of the week for this particular spell are Thursday (Jupiter's day) or Sunday (the sun's day).

Supplies and Directions: You will need a green seven-day jar candle. Sometimes these types of candles are called novenas. Gather a gold permanent marker or gold metallic nail polish to write your chosen prosperity symbol on the candle glass. (Seriously, nail polish works like a charm.) See page 57 for suggested prosperity symbols. Finally, you will need to plan for a space where this candle can safely burn for several days.

Center yourself and shift your mood to a positive and upbeat one. Here is that all-purpose candle blessing—with a slight adaptation. I am all about the ideas of adapt, improvise, and overcome! *Adapt* the blessing to fine-tune it, *improvise* with supplies (like nail polish) that you have on hand, and *overcome* any obstacle in your path.

Now empower and enchant the green jar candle:

As I hold this magickal jar candle in my hands
I empower it to send magick across the land.
Now burn with purpose both bright and true
May I be blessed in all that I do.

Place the decorated and enchanted jar candle in that chosen spot where it will be safe to continuously burn, and then light the candle. Now repeat the spell verse with intention and purpose.

For seven days this magick will build and grow
Crafting positive change as the candle glows.
It attracts to me expansion and success
As the candle burns I will surely be blessed.
May this magick manifest in the best possible way
Bringing happiness and gratitude to all of my days.

You may repeat this spell verse every day, at least once a day, while the jar candle is burning. Depending on your particular candle, this may be for five to nine days. Allow the candle to burn in a safe place until it goes out on its own. Finally, when the candle is completely burned out, close up the spell with these lines:

I embrace all of the possibilities
And as I do will it, then so shall it be.

Please note: The jar candle should stay continuously lit until it goes out on its own. If you need to move it to a safe location while you are out of the house, then do so. I often place the jar candle inside my large, deep cast-iron cauldron, then place the cauldron on my brick fireplace hearth. That way, should the candle get knocked over, it stays contained within the fireproof cauldron. Some practitioners place their jar candles inside of a sink or bathtub (away from drapes or shower curtains) or place the candle inside an unlit fireplace. You may have to move the candle around a bit for a few days. I have always found the magickal results to be well worth any minor inconvenience of plotting out a safe spot for the burning candle.

When you are finished with the jar candle, wash it out with saltwater to remove any lingering magick and recycle it.

Royal Blue Votive Candle Spell

The premier color associated with the planet Jupiter is royal blue. Some sources suggest purple and green as well, but I do like the idea of working with bright royal blue. Let's shake things up and be creative. Besides, that intense cobalt blue is a very powerful color, and it's different.

Timing: For best results, work this spell during a waxing moon phase. The corresponding day of the week for this particular spell is Thursday (Jupiter's day).

Supplies and Directions: One royal blue votive candle. You will need a tool to inscribe the votive candle with. You will also need a complementary candleholder. Votive candles require a cup-style holder, as they turn to liquid wax right away. Finally, you will want to set the votive (in the holder) upon a safe, flat surface for the candle to continue burning undisturbed for several hours.

Center yourself and shift your mood to a positive and upbeat one. Inscribe the candle with a Jupiter glyph (♃) then enchant the candle. Here is the candle blessing from the last spell, but it has been adapted slightly.

As I hold this royal blue spell candle in my hands
I enchant it to send magick out across the land.
Now burn with purpose both bright and true
May I be blessed in all that I do.

Place the inscribed and enchanted candle in the holder and light the candle, then repeat the spell verse with intention and purpose.

> By this burning candle in Jupiter's blue
> Prosperity and success will now ensue.
> By the element of fire this magick brings a change
> Success and prosperity are now within my range.
> May this magick manifest in the best possible way
> Bringing happiness and gratitude to all of my days.

Allow the spell candle to burn in a safe place until it goes out on its own. Votives generally take six to eight hours to burn. If you like, you can observe your candle's flame and see what it tells you about the progress of the spellwork.

Pyromancy:
Reading Your Spell Candle's Flames

Just as a candle cannot burn without fire,
men cannot live without a spiritual life.

BUDDHA

The dancing flame of a lit candle has a language all of its own and a divinatory technique to boot! Pyromancy, or divination by fire, is one of the earliest forms of divination. It is rumored that the followers of Hephastus, the Greek god of fire and the forge, as well as the priestesses of Athena, the Greek goddess of wisdom, practiced pyromancy.

All you need for pyromancy is to observe your spell candle in a quiet room that has no drafts. Then simply watch the flame of the spell candle and listen carefully for a while. This will clue you in on how your candle spell is working. At last, here we have the perfect reason to never leave a burning spell candle unattended again!

To begin the divination, sit back at least six feet from the candle flame and relax. Blink as you normally do—it's not a staring contest, it's supposed to be fun! Also, a lot of pyromancy is noting if the candle is "chattering," so listen carefully. It may take you a little practice, but honestly if you just pay attention and note how your spell candle is behaving, you are halfway there. Divination is wrought by noting the color, shape, and sounds of the spell candle's flames.

Here is a little pyromancy charm to help get you in the mood. As you begin to observe your burning spell candle, repeat this charm three times:

Candles that flicker and flames that dance
Show me the truth with a simple glance
By the sound of the flames, their shape and hue
Reveal to me how my magick will do.

Here is a quick list for you to use in deciphering your pyromancy. Spell candles that have...

- **sputtering and crackling candle flames** mean that someone else is affecting the spell's outcome
- **softly chattering candle flames** signify that your magick is affecting things on a personal level
- **loudly chattering candle flames** indicate that arguments are coming
- **strong and true candle flames** show that there is plenty of power and energy in your spell
- **jumping candle flames** represent that there is a lot of energy the spell has to work with and that raw emotions have been unleashed with the spell
- **weak candle flames** signify that there is resistance to your spellwork; cast again
- **bright blue candle flames** symbolize that a spirit is near

The Magick of Manifestation

The good news is that the moment you decide that
what you know is more important than what
you have been taught to believe, you will have
shifted your gears in your quest for abundance.
Success comes from within, not from without.

RALPH WALDO EMERSON

Casting prosperity spells and working candle magick are great beginnings, but you do have to back them up with physically working toward your goals if you want to see the magick manifest. No excuses, and armchair magicians will not be tolerated here.

It is time to get up and get to work on your successful future. Get up off your behind and work at making the changes you desire! Follow up your magick with action in the physical world. So yes, work those spells—and then put in job applications and follow up on leads. Then enchant your résumé and work some personal magick to make yourself stand out from other applicants at the interview. If you are self-employed, then work to promote your own small business or product and draw customers to your door.

Actively working in partnership with your magick on the physical plane will propel the magick forward and allow it to travel onward and outward, thus helping keep that positive energy in constant motion—and this helps to remove any resistance to its successful completion. After all, magick does manifest by following the path of least resistance.

Comprehending your dreams and goals and making the decision to go after them takes energy and motivation. Daring to work the magick to achieve the transformation is an adventure in and of itself. Following that up with action in the physical world keeps the transformation and positive change in motion. This then allows the magickal and physical energy to combine, allowing you to experience the manifestation of healthy abundance and prosperity.

In this third chapter we studied the energy and transformation that working with the element of fire can bring to your prosperity magick. Now you are motivated and ready to get to work on both the magickal and the mundane planes. Be enthusiastic and positive, and see what your magick and hard work will manifest into your world. Let your light shine!

Next up, we keep the bewitching flow going by diving into the magick of the element of water. Take a deep breath—here we go!

Chapter Four

WATER:
LETTING PROSPERITY FLOW

The Goddess tells us that wealth is everywhere and it
forever comes toward us like waves meeting the shore.
STACEY DEMARCO

AFTER WORKING OUR way through the first three chapters, we've got
the elemental principles of practical prosperity magick firmly in hand.
We have adjusted our mood and happiness and are building positive
thoughtforms. We have started to work our prosperity magick and are
allowing transformation and manifestation to bring illumination to our
existence. Now, we need to keep the magick and our prosperity flowing:
enter the element of water.

The magickal energy of prosperity can be described as fluid and
expansive. It will always find a way to manifest if a Witch is open to the
possibilities. Like the element of water, prosperity is without bounds.
There is always enough to go around. You just have to flow with it and
not fight against it. Prosperity *is* about energy flow. The truth is that this
type of elemental magick is not so much about money as it is about your
personal energy and how you interact with your environment. So here
is where we fine-tune the motion of that energy and keep it streaming
forward.

Immerse yourself into a new idea of prosperity and its magick.
Money is energy. It is even called currency. In economics, currency is
defined as a medium of exchanging values. When you get right down to

it, the word *current* refers to the movement of air, electricity, and water. Whether it is a trickle, a flow, a stream, or a flood of energy, it does have a circular pattern. This energetic currency is an important part of every-thing we do and experience. When you tap into it and work with it well, then happiness and satisfaction flow.

The God and Goddess control the flow of all things. So if you begin to treat the idea of prosperity as something divine and from the gods, you will then learn to run with it and trust in it. By working with the ele-ment of water in our prosperity magick, we can flow with this elemental energy to create the changes we desire.

Prosperous energy is meant to flow. For example, try visualizing this fluid energy as a body of water. If it sits still, with no movement or life, it stagnates. However, when there is motion and activity to this fluid energy, then it is oxygenated, healthy, and full of life. When things are flowing in your life, you feel as if you are on a roll. There is forward movement, and life seems magickal.

The more divine energy that circulates in your life, the happier and richer your life becomes—not only on a monetary level but on a spiri-tual level as well. We all have the opportunity to transform our lives and be prosperous. Laugh and enjoy your life. Splash, play, and allow divine joy to saturate you.

If you'd like to start working with that divine energy right now, say hello to two goddesses who are both associated with the element of water, prosperity, joy, and wealth: Lakshmi and Yemaya. Get to know them, work magick with them, and take pleasure in the joyful current they bring into your life.

Lakshmi:
Hindu Goddess of Prosperity and Wealth

You must be a lotus unfolding its petals
when the sun rises in the sky...

SAI BABA

Lakshmi is the Hindu goddess of both material and spiritual prosperity. She is the goddess of abundance, wealth, light, wisdom, fortune, fertility, generosity, courage, and good luck. Wow, that's one busy deity! Lakshmi is actively worshiped by millions of devotees today and is one of the most popular goddesses of the Hindu pantheon. She is considered to be the embodiment of grace and charm and is typically portrayed as a smiling, beautiful woman dressed in a red sari. Lakshmi has four arms and long, dark, wavy hair. She is depicted standing or dancing on top of a large lotus blossom that floats on the water. Her four arms are always in motion, and they are symbolic—one for each of the four directions—and show that she is always busy distributing wealth. They also represent her omnipotence.

The word *Lakshmi* is taken from the Sanskrit word *Laksya*, which means "goal." She is known as a household goddess or as a domestic deity. In some provinces, Lakshmi's festival occurs in autumn, when the full moon is the brightest—in other words, the harvest moon. On this night, she is believed to fly down on her sacred white owl to remove any poverty or stagnation from our lives. Lakshmi also uses her nighttime flights with the owl to shower her followers with abundance and wealth. Furthermore, October is generally considered to be sacred to Lakshmi, and at her Festival of Light, called Diwali, foods, sweets, and flowers such as marigolds are left as offerings.

This goddess of prosperity is different from other deities, as Lakshmi is associated with the element of water. Yes, you read that correctly: not the element of earth, *water*. While this fact may be surprising, considering her iconography it shouldn't be. You simply need to wrap your mind around a different pantheon. Water is life. Water brings fertility to the land and helps the crops grow and the plants bear fruit. Riches can be interpreted in many, many ways. For me, the water elemental association for Lakshmi works. After all, according to mythology, she was born from the "milky ocean," which helps explain her links to fertility magick, and Lakshmi is typically portrayed surrounded by water as she stands upon a mystical floating lotus blossom.

The lotus is a classic fertility symbol, as this blossom takes its strength from the water. This flower also represents spiritual power and personal growth, plus the lotus has a mystery to share. You will notice that while the lotus floats upon the water, it is not wet, which is a spiritual lesson of sorts from Lakshmi: to enjoy the wealth she brings but not to drown in any obsession with its obtainment.

Lakshmi is associated with two different creatures: the white owl, as mentioned above, for its vision and intelligence while she travels at night, and also white elephants. In India, elephants are a symbol of royal power, and a white elephant represents purity. Often Lakshmi is portrayed as flanked by a total of four white elephants. The pachyderms symbolize the four directions, sovereignty, and, best of all, they attract rain.

According to Hindu mythology, at one time all white elephants flew in the sky like clouds and were filled with water. Then one day a few accidentally fell to earth, losing their wings. These earthbound elephants have always wanted to rejoin their brothers in the sky who shower the earth with life-giving rain. So the closest the landbound elephants could do now was to use their trunks to spray water into the air to simulate rain. When they are portrayed with the goddess Lakshmi, they often have their trunks raised and are showering water/rain behind the goddess in a kind of salute.

For modern Witches today, Lakshmi is a mother goddess who is associated with the full moon phase. Whenever I have worked magick with Lakshmi, I have found that her magick manifests smoothly and in a soft, gentle way. Her influence is felt quickly, especially when you make sure to be generous to others in turn, as she is generous to you and yours.

As to how her magick manifests, think gentle nudges, good luck, positive energy, and magick that smoothly fills you up and brings prosperity into your life. She has a comforting presence and a gentle demeanor. Lakshmi responds particularly well to honest and honorable magickal requests concerning matters of prosperity and abundance that involve the well-being of the family.

For a Witch wanting to learn more about Lakshmi's magickal correspondences, all you have to do is take a look at the art and how she is represented. To begin with, her sari is red, and this color represents activity. She has golden embroidery on her costume, and the gold signifies fulfillment as well as material wealth. Lakshmi has a royal golden crown with rubies and wears strings of pearls and golden jewelry.

Lakshmi holds the promise of material fulfillment and contentment; to prove that, golden coins are always shown falling from her left hand. This gesture demonstrates that she provides wealth, prosperity, and contentment to all of her devotees.

Correspondences for Lakshmi

Goddess Aspect: Mother

Moon Phase: full

Planet: Venus

Element: water

Colors: red, gold

Flower: lotus, marigold

Crystals and Gems: low-grade rubies or pearls
(pearl jewelry works well)

Metal: gold

Associated Animals: white owl, white elephant

Other Items: coins, especially gold

Magickal Goals: prosperity, abundance, fertility, generosity

A Spell for Prosperity with Lakshmi

Timing: Work the spell during a waxing moon or on the night of a full moon.

Suggested Supplies and Directions: For this spell, obtain a picture of the goddess Lakshmi. Do an image search and print a picture of her that appeals to you. For example, I found a pretty one, printed it out, and put it in a small frame so I could use it as a focal point in my magickal workspace. You will want to add a golden coin or dollar bill to the spell, plus two small candles, one red and one gold, with two coordinating candleholders. You'll also need a small dish of water and a few marigold flowers from the garden, or a dried lotus blossom. (Lotus pods are easily found at the arts and crafts store.)

Refer to the previous correspondence chart for more ideas, and put some effort into making the altar setup as pretty as you can. Arrange the accoutrements around the central image of Lakshmi in a way that pleases you.

Traditionally, any requests made to Lakshmi are started by repeating the phrase "Om Ganesha" three times. Ganesha is the elephant-headed deity who is a remover of obstacles and is honored at the opening of rituals and ceremonies. Then, after Ganesha's invocation, you may proceed with the spell. Also in ritual, Lakshmi is addressed as "maha Lakshmi." Why, you may ask? Because *maha* means "great." It is a way of showing respect and love to Lakshmi.

To begin, ground and center yourself, and study her image carefully. Allow her smiling face to fill you up with warmth and happiness. Then light the red and the gold candle. Now repeat the invocation and spell verse:

Om Ganesha

Om Ganesha

Om Ganesha

Beautiful dancing goddess of wealth, luck, and prosperity,

Grant to me good fortune. I request your help, maha Lakshmi.

Please let golden coins, extra cash, and abundance flow my way.

Surround me with your loving presence, blessing me night and day.

I will return this gentle kindness that you have shown to me

By helping others when I can; as I will, so mote it be.

Allow the spell candles to burn until they go out on their own. Be sure to keep an eye on them. Leave the altar setup and her picture in place for one week, freshening the flowers and water as you need to. If you like, you may relight new small candles to her every day during the week. When the abundance starts to flow into your life, remember to be generous, in turn, to others.

Blessed be!

Yemaya:
The Goddess of the Seven Seas

Water is the driving force of all nature.

LEONARDO DA VINCI

Yemaya is the orisha of the sea and rivers. She is a nature spirit often depicted as a beautiful black mermaid and known for her generosity, protection of women, kindness, and her loving influences. Her worship originated in Africa as a river goddess of the Yoruba in Nigeria. She gave birth to the sun and moon and all of the waters; she is called the Mother of Fishes and a fertility goddess. Her devotees brought her with them when they were brought to foreign lands as captives. Yemaya protected them and offered them hope. Eventually Yemaya's worship spread to the Caribbean and Brazil.

Yemaya has many names and titles. Variations of her name include Yemaja, Yemanja, Iemanja, Janaina, La Sirène, and Yemanya. She is also called Stella Maris, the Star of the Sea, Our Lady of Regla, and the Mother of Fishes. Yemaya symbolizes the ebb and flow of life; just like the ocean, she can help us move easily through our lives and she can assist with loving, positive change.

As her worship spread, Yemaya adapted and took on different forms in different cultures. In Voodoo she is seen as a moon goddess. In Santeria she is the mother of all living things as well as the goddess of the seven seas. In Brazil she is honored at the summer solstice as the patroness of fisherman and the Mother of the Oceans. On New Year's Eve in Rio de Janeiro, people gather seaside all dressed in white to greet the new year and pay homage to the goddess of the sea. They create altars on the beach with candles, watch fireworks, and at midnight launch wooden toy boats or toss white flowers into the ocean as offerings for the goddess, with the hope that "Iemanja" will grant their request.

Yemaya's ocean domain is thought to be in the upper levels of the sea where the sunlight warms the water, causing it to evaporate. This moisture is carried to the land by her daughter Oya, the wind, where it billows into clouds and makes rain for the crops.

Correspondences for Yemaya

Goddess Aspect: Mother

Moon Phase: crescent, full

Planet: Neptune

Element: water

Colors: blue, white, silver

Flower: white rose

Crystals and Gems: turquoise, coral, pearls

Associated Animals: sea birds, dolphins, fish

Symbols: six-pointed star, seashells (especially cowrie)

Number: seven (the seven seas)

Offerings: white roses, blue and clear glass beads, melon, small wooden boats, copper pennies, molasses

Magickal Goals: generosity, fertility, good luck, success

Sea and River Magick: Calling on Yemaya for Success

When you work with Yemaya, you will need an offering. This should be an item that the goddess enjoys or is associated with. And in the truest sense of the word, you will offer it to her as a gift and not take it back.

You will need to trust that she will do with it as she sees fit. I have seen it myself firsthand. Last year when I was in Florida on an anniversary trip with my husband, we were walking on the beach at sunrise. I came across several white roses tied in blue ribbons that had washed up in the tide along one stretch of the beach. My husband bent down to pick up a rose, and I snagged his hand before he could touch it.

"You are going to want to leave that alone," I quietly suggested.

He snatched his hand back, looked at me carefully, and simply asked, "Witch stuff?"

I looked a little farther up the beach and discovered the remains of an altar dug out in the sand, with a few stubs of candles left behind. I pointed it out to him, and in unspoken agreement we left those beautiful roses as they were. When we came back that way, retracing our steps an hour later, the roses were all swept out to sea again, and the candle stubs and sand altar had been taken down.

Timing, Supplies, and Directions: For best results, work this spell during a waxing moon. As the moon grows, so too will your prosperity.

To work this spell, you're going to need to be in a very specific place by the water's edge. Also, you are going to be wading into the water, so be careful and don't go out too far; ankle- to knee-deep is fine. Stay out of dangerous tides or strong currents. If you need to stay on the riverbank or the surf's edge, out of the water, that's fine—just be sure you are able to toss the floral offering well out there and into the water.

For your floral offering you will need seven fresh white roses tied with blue ribbon. Yes, they have to be real flowers. The ribbon does not need to be large; keep it small and tie it in a small bow. I'd recommend a ¼-inch satin blue ribbon, just enough to tie the flowers together. Keep it as simple and as biodegradable as possible.

Carefully wade into the water and wait for seven waves to splash your legs, then give the bouquet to Yemaya by tossing the bouquet gently out and into the water. (The spell is adaptable for both the river or the sea.)

After you have given her the bouquet, request her assistance with the following spell verse:

> *Beautiful goddess Yemaya, star of the sea*
> *Accept my heartfelt offering and hear my plea.*
> *Seven roses I offer to you upon the water's waves*
> *Please send success into my life in many wonderful ways.*
> *By the element of water, this spell is cast*
> *Prosperity flows to me and will surely last!*

Let the roses float or sink as they may; leave them for Yemaya. Wade back out of the water and onto the shore, then make your way home.

If you like, once you are home, you can back up your magick with a blue or white floating candle. Light the candle and float it in a clear glass bowl. Use the spell verse from above; simply change the third line to say, "Seven roses I've offered you upon the water's waves…" Finish the rest of the spell as written, and you are all set. Allow the floating spell candle to burn out in a safe place, then clean up.

No Access to the Ocean?
No Problem!

It is a wise person that adapts
themselves to all contingencies;
it's the fool who always struggles like
a swimmer against the current.

AUTHOR UNKNOWN

Now if, for some reason, you do not have access to an ocean or a river, you can still work with Yemaya. Where I live, the two largest rivers on the continent meet: the Mississippi and the Missouri Rivers. Around here one cannot wade into the river water; the river currents are swift and dangerous. If I am lucky, I get to the ocean once every couple of years…so what's a Witch to do? Why, I thought you would never ask. For Witches, adaptability and ingenuity are the names of the game.

I work with Yemaya in my backyard gardens quite often. We know she likes flowers, so I have tried working with her here at home, and it works out very well. I have successfully called on her during a drought to bless the yard, neighborhood, and county with much-needed rain. And yes, I am very cautious when it comes to working weather magick, in case you wondered.

However, Yemaya is also terrific when it comes to boosting your spirituality, and she can be very generous to Witches who approach her correctly and reverently with the appropriate offering.

I have found that Yemaya can help me to reconnect to the Divine. Yemaya can also bless you with a lovely generosity of spirit. This spiritual boost can help you to stay positive and work with the flow of the magick that is all around you. If this sounds like something you would like to explore, check out this next spell.

Yemaya's Spiritual Boost Spell

Timing: For best results, work this spell during a waxing moon. As the moon grows, so too will your connection to the goddess.

Supplies:
- one clear glass bowl filled with water
- a blue or white flower-shaped floating candle
- seashells (any kind; however, conch and cowrie are her favorites)
- blue, clear, and white glass beads or flat-bottomed glass marbles or glass gems (check the local arts and crafts stores for these glass gems)
- a biodegradable offering (a few very thin slices of melon are perfect)

Directions: As the moon rises, place the water-filled bowl in a spot in your garden where it will catch the moon's light. Take a few moments to make the altar area look pretty. Scatter some of those gems or glass marbles at the bottom of the bowl or around the outside. Arrange the shells around the outside of the bowl. Place the melon on a little dish and set it to the side.

Light the floating candle, and repeat the following spell verse:

Yemaya, I call on you as the moon waxes to full
May the candlelight bless this water so calm, clear, and cool.
Star of the Sea, your lovely magick is everywhere
May it manifest now by fire, water, and air.

Now take the plated offering of melon and set it out in the garden. As you do, say these lines:

Generosity of the spirit I am casting for this night
Lady, I offer you a gift; may it be pleasing in your sight.

Reverently place the offering dish in the garden. Close up the spell by returning to your altar. Then say:

The spell is now cast by my own hand
May it manifest across my land.

Keeping the candle attended, allow the floating candle to burn out. If you need to move it indoors to finish, do so. When the candle is spent, pour the water from the bowl out on the earth and clean up your other spell components.

Permit nature to reclaim the little slices of melon as it sees fit; do not take them back or remove them! The birds or the insects will be happy with them; let nature take its course. When the melon is gone from your gardens, remove the plate and wash it, saving it for another time.

May Yemaya bless you with a renewed sense of spirituality and magickal purpose.

The Nine of Cups card from Witches Tarot

Wish Fulfillment

Our deepest wishes are whispers
of our authentic selves.

SARAH BAN BREATHNACH

Here is another pretty spell that works with floating candles, this time with tarot imagery as well.

The Nine of Cups is an enchanting card. In my *Witches Tarot*, the card shows nine silver cups arranged in an arc across a covered banquet table. Behind the table, a pretty woman wearing a bright blue and green gown stands, smiling contentedly and pouring wine into one of the cups, as if to welcome you to a feast. The hostess has mystical peacock feathers and a blue flower in her hair, with a necklace containing nine stones around her throat.

The tablecloth is pale aqua blue, and there are starfish and shells worked into the cloth's design for a visual link to the element of water. An arrangement of pineapples, grapes, apples, and a pumpkin are displayed artfully on the table as if a celebration is about to occur. The pineapple is a classic symbol of hospitality. The pumpkin, apples, and grapes speak of the harvest season's bounty, and the pumpkin is associated with the moon and the element of water. In the background, a cauldron—classic symbol of the Goddess—is simmering over a hearth fire.

When the Nine of Cups turns up in a tarot reading, it symbolizes hospitality, abundance, and celebrations. It is also has a reputation as being the "wishes granted" card. This card's symbolism is all about dreams coming true, achieving your goals, and enjoying the pleasures of life. There is happiness and financial security, and your heart's desire can be fulfilled. The Nine of Cups is a perfect card for water-aligned prosperity magick, as this card illustrates that what we visualize will come to pass.

Nine of Cups Tarot Spell

Timing: Work this spell in a waxing moon phase. As the moon grows, so will your dreams. The most opportune time to work this spell would be on a Friday—a Venus day. This is a happy day filled with loving emotions and is just the ticket for this particular work.

Supplies: For this simple elemental spell, you will only need a few items: a blue floating candle, a lighter, a glass bowl filled with clean water, the Nine of Cups card from your tarot deck, and a safe, flat surface.

Directions: Place the water-filled bowl and the tarot card upon the altar. Light the floating candle and focus on that tarot card. Visualize the goals that you have for yourself. See yourself as happy and prosperous—your dreams and wishes are coming true. Then repeat the spell verse three times:

> *The Nine of Cups card will now be for me*
> *A lovely symbol for prosperity.*
> *My dreams and wishes will be granted, this much is true*
> *This magick begins with a floating candle of blue.*

Close up the spell with these lines:

> *For the good of all, with harm to none*
> *By tarot's magick, this spell is done!*

Allow the floating candle to burn out in a safe place. When it is finished, pour the water from the bowl out on the earth and clean up. Place the Nine of Cups card under your pillow. More information about the spellwork may be revealed in your dreams. You may also choose to keep the Nine of Cups card out for a few days to look at and remind you of your magick, or you may return it to the tarot deck. The choice is yours.

Feng Shui and Prosperity with Water

No human being, however great or
powerful, was ever so free as a fish.

JOHN RUSKIN

To close up this water-themed chapter, I thought it would be fun to explore working with feng shui and its marvelous energies to add prosperity to your home environment. In feng shui traditions, prosperity can be increased by incorporating moving water into your home, as adding moving water to the home environment is considered to be a "cure." Water embodies the yin (feminine) energy; it is calm, soothing, and neutral. The traditional feng shui colors for this watery energy are black and blue. One of the simplest ways to do this is to set up a pretty indoor tabletop fountain.

Indoor fountains are among the more popular feng shui water cures. However, with my little calico kitty familiar living in the house, I put the kibosh on the idea of an indoor fountain, no matter how small or pretty. Our cat would use that fountain as a drinking bowl, no doubt about it, so this wasn't an option for me. What caught my imagination instead was the feng shui practice of adding a compact aquarium. Aquariums are considered to be auspicious in feng shui practices.

If you'd like to incorporate this clever feng shui trick, add a small aquarium to the southeast corner of your home or home office. A small aquarium is actually preferred in feng shui. The southeast area is considered a prime location because the southeast corner of a room or home is designated as the wealth and abundance area. However, if the southeast corner is not a viable option for you, never fear: there are other options. For example, the north area symbolizes career and the east is for health and family.

In feng shui, the element of water symbolizes nourishment, wealth, and the flow of life. Since the pumps inside of the aquarium keep the water clean and circulating, this creates healthy energy as well as attracts new and positive chi, or energy. Bottom line: the circulating, moving water inside the aquarium will encourage the increased flow of prosperity into the home.

Aquariums with fish represent a combination of water energy and living energy. In feng shui, fish are considered symbols of wealth and happiness. It is interesting that the number of fish inside the aquarium can have a symbolic meaning as well. For example, three fish symbolize growth and development. Six fish represent wealth and prosperity. Eight fish stand for money and financial stability. Finally, nine fish signify a long, happy life.

If you go for nine fish, then it is suggested that eight be golden-orange while one is black. The reason is that the golden fish attract prosperity, and the black fish will pick up and get rid of any negativity in the home. No matter how many fish you choose to add to your aquarium, it is recommended that they be bright and colorful.

You can incorporate all five of the feng shui elements quite easily with an aquarium. In feng shui traditions, the five elements are water, wood, metal, earth, and fire. The water, obviously, is in the aquarium tank; the wood is the plants in the aquarium. Metal can be incorporated by using white or gray rocks in the aquarium or a iron stand to hold the tank. To incorporate earth you have the gravel at the bottom of the tank, and the element of fire can be added by the light for the tank and by adding fish that are red, orange, or yellow.

I liked this idea so much that I had my husband dig out our little fish tank and stand and add it into my home office. I set it up in the southeast corner, and it is very soothing and pretty to watch the fish swim around. Also, the cat loves it—built-in kitty entertainment!

Be sure to keep your aquarium in good working order, with a lid that closes securely, and keep your aquarium clean. If you want to try this pretty feng shui cure for increasing prosperity in your home or home office, here is a spell to bless your new aquarium.

A Witchy Blessing for Your Aquarium

Hold your hands above your newly completed aquarium. Watch the fish swim around for a few moments. Center yourself and build up some positive, life-affirming thoughtforms. Raise up your personal energy and let it flow from your hands to the aquarium, then say:

> As the aquarium's water bubbles, cycles, and flows
> Prosperity now comes to me, this I surely do know.
> Little fish, swim about and add your positive chi
> Water flow, work your magick and send success to me!
> By feng shui energy this watery spell is cast
> Wash over me with riches and make the magick last.

Chapter Five

ATTRACTING ABUNDANCE

Abundance is not something we acquire.
It is something we tune in to.

WAYNE DYER

SO WHY IS a chapter on attracting abundance in the center of the book? Well, the answer is pretty simple. For the past four chapters, for the most part we have been working on active and projective magickal practices where you set out to actively create a change. This required rebuilding your magickal foundation and adjusting your energetic and emotional vibration. Then we started enthusiastically working with elemental spells to get that prosperous energy rolling.

When it comes to active and projective magickal energies, you go after your goals. You make the positive change happen. Active and projective energy requires confidence. We all have the ability to create abundance; what is important to remember is that you must have the ability to *do*, not just try. You have to be persistent and eager to take a chance on improving your world. This requires both heart and personal will to make things change.

With receptive and magnetic energies, you will learn to attract prosperity and healthy abundance into your life. You will magnetize the energy, draw it in, and allow it to happen. Receptive and magnetic energies require openness, vulnerability, trust, patience, nurturing, and a willingness to relax and accept.

Personally, my biggest challenge is to be receptive and to *allow* when it comes to spellcraft. I am impatient by nature and would much rather dive in and do than be patient and allow. But everyone needs to shake things up and learn new things. As Richard Bach says, you teach best what you most need to learn.

Abundance:
What Is It Really and How Do I Get Me Some?

Abundance is about being rich,
with or without money.

SUZE ORMAN

Abundance means different things to different people. Abundance can be financial, physical, emotional, or spiritual. The word *abundance* is often used interchangeably with prosperity, but are they really the same thing? To be honest, abundance does not equal money; money is just a symbol. Money is energy, and yes, if you are in a healthy relationship with money, its energy should be respected and appreciated.

However, in truth, abundance is a state of mind, a way of thinking, a way of living and being. Abundance encompasses not just cash but all forms of wealth. And by wealth I mean a spilling over of love, peace, health, joy, and happiness.

Think of it this way: the word *abundance* comes from the Latin *abundare*, which means "to overflow." Today, abundance is defined as an ample profusion, wealth, or plenty.

What is important to remember is that you are the source of your own abundance. Focus on what your magickal goals are and draw them right to yourself. Those thoughts that are laced with magickal intention energize your positive thoughtforms and push your magick out into the world. There they begin to manifest and create the positive changes that you desire.

In essence, this is a more intimate way of working with the Hermetic principles of polarity and gender. In this chapter, you will look at both the masculine and feminine energies and work to put them in a healthy balance, keeping in mind that your energies should be calm, neutral, and centered. The more in control you are, the easier your magick will create the changes that you are working toward and thinking about. Hold all of these thoughts firmly in your mind because *thoughts create.* They have substance and, bottom line, thoughts are magnetic.

How to Become Magnetic:
Embrace Your Receptive Energies

I believe that there is a subtle magnetism
in Nature, which, if we unconsciously
yield to it, will direct us aright.

HENRY DAVID THOREAU

Magnetic powers are considered to be receptive energies. To attract healthy abundance into your life is to become magnetic to prosperity, drawing in abundance. Then you can allow that abundant and successful energy to overflow into your world. This type of receptive energy is classified as feminine, as it draws toward itself what it most desires. And every person, male or female, is a fabulous blending and mixture of both masculine/projective and feminine/receptive energies.

When an individual is magnetic, they possess an extraordinary power to attract. They can attract whatever they most want and are willing to work for—a positive change, prosperity, healthy abundance…whatever they most desire. Witches simply take the idea of magnetism and tap into this natural power, shaping it with purpose and then allowing it to ripple out into their lives.

These receptive and magnetic forces can be tapped into quite easily, as they are natural forces. Magnetism is a physical phenomenon. This phenomenon involves a science that deals with fields of force, or energy (as in one is attracted to another). Magnetism is also defined as the ability to attract or to charm. If a situation is "charmed," then it has been affected by magick, and in this case the abundance and prosperity that you desire can be drawn more easily to you.

This then leads us to a discussion of receptive power. To be receptive is to be able to receive, to draw in, to be open and responsive. Receptive power is part of the divine feminine, and being receptive is a gift from the Goddess. Some folks hear the word *receptive* and they think it means weak or submissive, but they are mistaken. Receptive power is, in fact, magnetic, compelling, and intensely fascinating.

If you refer once again to the illustration of the Magician tarot card on page 16, you will see that this archetypal image is not only manifesting his desire, he also is claiming his own personal power. The Magician is drawing in and creating a magickal change.

Magick exists. You will find that power when you truly see and live the truth of who you are. As a magickal practitioner, it is time to focus your power and accept that you are wise and spiritual. You are now becoming more open, or "receptive," and this makes you optimistic and therefore more powerful. With this comes confidence and a generosity of spirit, allowing you to transform your reality in wonderful ways.

To be receptive is to be open to all of the enchanting possibilities that are out there. Experience the manifestation of your goals, and allow this energy to flow toward yourself with joy.

Attracting Abundance

Abundance is, in large part, an attitude.

SUE PATTON THOELE

The overflowing cornucopia is an ancient symbol for prosperity and abundance. This is a popular and traditional decoration for celebrating the wealth of nature at the harvest. *Cornucopia* literally means "horn of plenty." The word itself comes from the root words *cornu*, which means "horn," and *copia*, meaning—you guessed it—"plenty." The symbol has been around since the fifth century BCE.

According to mythology, when the god Zeus was a toddler, he was playing with his goat nursemaid named Almathea. Little Zeus was so strong that he accidentally broke off one of her horns. In apology he gave her back the horn, only now it had the power to grant whoever held it whatever they wished for. Other versions of the story say that Almathea broke off the horn herself and filled it full of food for Zeus as a gift. To show his appreciation, Zeus placed his nursemaid in the sky, and she became the constellation of Capricorn.

The goat's horn overflowing with fruit and grain was a popular image in ancient times on both Greek and Roman coins. Besides Zeus and his goat nursemaid, other deities associated with the horn of plenty were the Roman goddesses Fortuna, Pax, and Abuntania.

The following cornucopia spell can be worked at any time of the year; however, astrological timing is crucial for this ritual. Working in harmony with the tides of the moon and the most opportune days of the week will help this magick manifest more easily.

A Cornucopia Spell

Timing:

> *Moon Phase:* waxing moon
>
> *Most Opportune Day:* Thursday (prosperity and abundance)

Supplies:

> *Candle:* green votive candle, a votive cup
>
> *Stone:* lodestone
>
> *Additional Supplies:* a lighter or matches, one 8.5 by 11-inch sheet of heavy green or gold cardstock (check your scrapbook supplies), tape, a few silver and gold coins, three one-dollar bills, a ten-dollar gift card to a local grocery store (to represent food)

Directions: Set up your work area and choose a safe spot to allow the votive candle to burn undisturbed. It can burn up to eight hours.

Once you are set up and have your supplies gathered, put yourself into a proper frame of mind: receptive, optimistic, and focused. Begin by rolling the heavy paper into a cone shape and securing the paper cone with a few pieces of tape. This cone becomes your cornucopia. (If you own a cornucopia basket, you may certainly use that.)

As you roll the paper into a cone shape, say the following:

> *By the magickal waxing moon so bright*
> *A cornucopia is made this night.*

Now empower/bless the green candle, as was described for you in chapter 3, and say:

> *As I hold this green votive spell candle in my hands*
> *I enchant it to send abundance across the land.*

Place the votive in the candleholder and light it. Once it is burning well, then continue by saying reverently and with intention:

Now burn with purpose both bright and true
May I be blessed in all that I do.

Now add the lodestone, the gift card, the coins, and the three dollar bills to the paper cornucopia. Place the cornucopia in the center of your work space and next to the green candle. Hold your hands above the filled cornucopia and say:

The cornucopia is an ancient symbol of plenty
Adding a lodestone inside will help to draw fortune quickly.
Now filled with food, coins, and dollar bills counting three
This spell will attract abundance swiftly to me!
May this manifest in the best possible way
Bringing healthy abundance to all of my days.

Allow the green candle to burn out in a safe place. Leave the cash and gift card in the cornucopia for a full month. During this time, whenever you have an extra buck or change, add it to the cornucopia. If you need to, you can transfer the extra change to a jar; just leave the cornucopia with the original money right next to it.

After the month has ended, put the extra gathered money back in your bank account. As for the grocery store gift card, you have a couple of options. Keep it for an emergency or, better yet, give it to someone who you know could use it—a college student, someone just starting out in their first apartment, or a friend struggling to make ends meet. Remember to give so that you can, in turn, abundantly receive!

The Wheel of the Year card from Witches Tarot

Fortuna:
Goddess of Abundance

There is something in a woman
beyond all human delight,
a magnetic virtue, a charming quality,
an occult and powerful motive.

ROBERT BURTON

The Roman goddess Fortuna was previously mentioned in the information about the cornucopia. Fortuna is the daughter of Jupiter. The Greeks knew her as Tyche. A very popular deity before the advent of Christianity, Fortuna is associated with luck, fate, abundance, destiny, and oracles. It is thought there were more temples to Fortuna in old Rome than any other god of the time. Her festival day was June 24, and she was depicted as a winged goddess standing upon a globe with a wheel nearby and holding both a cornucopia and a ship's rudder.

It is through her symbols that we learn more about Fortuna. The globe showed that her influence was felt everywhere in the world. The cornucopia identified her as a giver of abundance. The cornucopia speaks to her beginnings as a fertility goddess, and she blessed gardens with abundant crops. The ship's rudder symbolized that she was the controller of destinies and that she could steer your course through the ups and downs of life. Fortuna was also depicted with an eight-spoked wheel, and this literally would be the original Wheel of Fortune.

The Wheel of Fortune card in the Major Arcana is sometimes called the Wheel of the Year, as it symbolizes the passage of time. The goddess Fortuna is the one who turns the wheel. She is the keeper of time and the cycles of nature, and she is the one who steers us through the waters of life. Did you ever notice how the wheel in the card resembles a ship's wheel?

In my *Witches Tarot*, the Wheel of the Year card is rightly associated with the goddess Fortuna. This major arcana card symbolizes the magick of the four seasons and the energies of the wheel of the year. When this card turns up in a tarot reading, it is a symbol of good fortune and a message to work with, not against, the energies and cycles of nature that are currently around you. Rest and introspection in the winter; new beginnings, growth, and opportunities in the spring. Summer brings energy, excitement, bounty, and vibrancy, while autumn brings abundance and reminds us to prepare, to gather in, and to remember. Expect there to be change, as all of life is forever transforming and growing. This card classically represents good luck, opportunity, and a fortuitous event.

A Tarot Spell with Fortuna

Here is the perfect opportunity to get to know Fortuna a little better while working magick with the classic images found in the tarot deck.

Timing and Supplies:

    Moon Phase: waxing moon

    Planetary Association: Jupiter

    Day of the Week: Thursday (Jupiter's day)

    Tarot Card Association: The Wheel of the Year/Wheel of Fortune

    Stone: lodestone

    Candle Color: green (may be a votive, taper, or mini spell candle)

    Other Supplies: a coordinating candleholder, a straight pin or your boline (to inscribe the candle), matches or a lighter

Directions: Set up this spell on your work area or altar. Prop the Wheel of the Year/Wheel of Fortune card up on the lodestone. Take a moment and center yourself. Put your frame of mind into a neutral and receptive state. Build some positive thoughtforms. If you like, you can inscribe the green candle with Fortuna's eight-spoked wheel. While you engrave the candle, visualize healthy abundance coming to you in a wonderful variety of ways. Now empower the green candle by saying:

> As I engrave this green candle in my hands
> It will attract abundance across the land.

Place the inscribed green candle in its holder and light it. Once it is burning well, then continue by saying reverently and with intention:

> Now burn with purpose both bright and true
> May I be blessed in all that I do.

When you are ready, repeat the spell verse:

> Lady Fortuna, please hear my call
> In the winter, spring, summer, and fall.
> While the lodestone attracts abundance and prosperity
> May the Wheel of Fortune always turn in favor for me.
> As Fortuna's magick spins out and about
> It pulls good fortune in and keeps bad luck out.
> For the good of all, with harm to none
> By tarot's magick, this spell is done!

Leave the tarot card and lodestone in place for as long as the candle burns, and be sure to keep an eye on that spell candle! Then, when the candle is spent, return the card to the deck and pocket the lodestone.

May Fortuna smile upon you!

Lodestone Magick and Magnetic Sand

The world is your mirror and your mind is a magnet.
What you perceive in this world is largely a
reflection of your own attitudes and beliefs...
Think and act and talk with enthusiasm
and you will attract positive results.

MICHAEL LEBEUF

Lodestones, or magnetic iron ore, are an interesting new trick to add to your witchy repertoire. They attract prosperity, success, and good fortune. Lodestones have the planetary correspondence of both Mars and Venus. They can also be classified as having a gender, which may explain the Mars/Venus planetary association. The rounded lodestones are considered feminine, while phallic-shaped lodestones are identified as masculine. When it comes to magick, lodestones are typically carried in pairs—one to attract good luck and prosperity, and the other to repel bad luck and negativity.

Lodestones (also called magnetite) are a wonderful and beneficial magickal tool. They are traditionally tucked into cash-register drawers to attract money and customers, and they are often worked into charm bags for all of the purposes listed above. Interestingly, lodestones will increase the power of any other types of spellcasting such as healing, love, friendship, or protection. Bottom line: lodestones are for attraction.

Now, just to keep things interesting, lodestones themselves are thought to be alive and have memories, and they are traditionally "fed" with gold or silver magnetic sand. No kidding. Now, if you are like me, my first thought was, what will I do with the leftover magnetic sand?

Well, you can use magnetic sand to complement other prosperity talismans or amulets as well. Sand empowers and boosts good luck amulets such as horseshoes, silver charms, trinkets, or other lucky charms. You may also roll the magnetic sand on prosperity spell candles, sprinkle it around the candle base, or even use it to draw a magick circle on the ground. Magnetic sand is often dusted across thresholds to invite good fortune and prosperity to your home or business, and it also attracts new friends and welcomes friends and family.

This information tickled my imagination. I had never worked with magnetic sand or raw lodestones before. So, in an effort to teach myself something new and then share it with my readers, I decided to try this out for myself. Excitedly, I got online and tracked down green lodestones and gold magnetic sand.

> **Practical Magick Note:** Lodestones are naturally black or dark gray. Sometimes they are painted in various colors. I went with green lodestones for my spells because I thought they were pretty. I also chose the gold magnetic sand as the color gold corresponds to wealth, the sun, and success. To me this seemed the most complementary way to go. However, if you prefer to work with silver magnetic sand, natural colored lodestones, or what you have on hand, then go for it.

When my order arrived, I was shocked at how heavy that little bag of sand was. I also quickly discovered that when I handled the sand, it was so fine that a gold metallic dust went all over my work surface and my hands, so I simply rubbed the metallic dust all over the spell candles and the charm bag I was preparing. Afterwards, I cleaned any lingering metallic dust from the altar with a damp cloth, otherwise I would have had little gold kitty pawprints all over my house. Brianna, my calico cat, loves to watch over any spell experiments, just as a proper familiar should. When she started swiping her paws through that sandy gold dust, I knew I'd better clean it up fast.

Thus began my experiments with lodestones and magnetic sand. It was fun, and here are a few of the best spells that I came up with.

Lodestone and Magnetic Sand Charm Bag

Timing:

> *Day of the Week:* Thursday (Jupiter's day) for prosperity and abundance or Sunday (sun's day) for wealth, fame, and success

> *Moon Phase:* first quarter and waxing (about seven days before the full moon)

Supplies:

- a safe, flat surface
- a 3-inch square of plain white paper
- blue ink pen (blue is a Jupiter color)
- green spell candle and complementary holder
- 2 small green lodestones
- gold magnetic sand
- tape
- lighter or matches
- green organza favor bag or a 4-inch square of green cotton fabric
- a gold dollar coin
- green ribbon

Directions:

Write the words *positive abundance and prosperity* in the center of the slip of paper. Fold up the edges toward the center so it creates a pocket. Set this aside so it is ready to go. Light the candle and then add the two lodestones and a pinch of sand to the paper pocket. Fold it up carefully and seal it closed with a bit of tape so it stays nice and neat. If you end up with golden dust on your fingers from the sand, rub it onto the spell candle.

Now you are ready to begin. Here is the spell verse to empower the charm bag:

> By this green spell candle's flickering light
> My wealth begins to increase on this night.

Place the sealed packet of lodestones and sand gently inside of the charm bag. Now say:

> These two lodestones will attract healthy abundance to me
> A pinch of magnetic sand allows the lodestones to feed.

Next add the gold coin and tie the sachet bag closed with the green ribbon. Close up the spell verse by saying:

> Now add a gold coin for wealth and prosperity
> Then tie the charm bag closed with a ribbon of green.
> By the power of the waxing moon so bright
> I conjure to increase my fortune tonight.

Place the charm bag next to the spell candle, keeping it a safe distance from the flame. Allow the spell candle to burn out in a safe place. Once the candle is spent, the charm bag is ready to go. You may keep the charm bag with you until the full moon. On the night of the full moon, allow some of the moonlight to fall upon the charm bag. Tuck the bag in your pocket, purse, or desk at work. You may recharge the bag at any following full moon.

Variations and Notes:

In some forms of American folk magick, the lodestones are placed in a red flannel bag for prosperity. No matter what type of bag you eventually use, you can certainly add a little good luck charm to the green ribbon. I tend to pick up packages of those little organza favor bags at the arts and crafts store—look in the bridal section. The organza favor bags have a drawstring and come in a rainbow of colors.

For extra oomph, set a High John the Conqueror root next to the spell candle or a Fourth Pentacle of Jupiter talisman next to the charm bag while the spell candle burns. (There will be more information on coins, good luck charms, and the Fourth Pentacle of Jupiter in the following chapters.)

A Lodestone Witch-Jar Spell That You Can Personalize

This next spell was inspired by cleaning up the kitchen, of all things. I was washing dishes—yes, I do them by hand—and was cleaning out an empty jelly jar to be recycled. Suddenly it dawned on me that it could make a nice Witch jar for spells. I started imagining all of the cool things I could do with that jar for prosperity magick…so with my imagination running, I washed the jar and lid out thoroughly and set it to air dry, and then started to plot and plan. Here is what I conjured up.

Supplies:
- slip of paper
- blue ink pen
- glass canning jar with a lid or recycle an old jelly jar and lid
- 2 lodestones
- gold metallic sand (enough to cover the bottom of the jar)
- ¼ cup gold craft glitter (check the arts and crafts store)
- three different colored coins such as a gold, a silver, and a copper-colored coin
- green satin ribbon 12 inches in length

Directions:

Personalize this to your specific needs. Write one of the following lines on the slip of paper: *To draw prosperity and healthy abundance into my life. To draw opportunities for a new, better job. To draw more customers to my business. To increase sales.* You get the idea. Now lay that paper in the bottom of the jar, then carefully add two lodestones. Sprinkle gold magnetic sand over the lodestones and the paper, covering the bottom of the jar with sand. Next, add a layer of gold glitter, and then finally place the three different coins in the jar. (You will want to leave at least three-quarters of the jar empty.) Now carefully close up the jar and repeat the spell verse:

> *Layer upon layer this enchantment does build*
> *Now this canning jar with my magick I do fill.*
> *Two green lodestones to attract and sand to feed*
> *And coins of different colors numbering three.*
> *With this magick I now draw extra cash to this spell jar*
> *Opportunities for money will come from near and far.*

Finally, seal the spell jar by tying a green satin ribbon around its neck. As you do, say the following lines:

> *By the power of the earth this spell I cast*
> *May I be successful and my magick last.*

Set the pretty jar in a place where you can see it every day. Any time you have an extra dollar, roll it up and add it to the jar. Keep at it. You can use that jar for emergency funds or eventually add it back into your bank account after six months.

Manifesting Abundance and Success

Success is focusing the full power of all you are
on what you have a burning desire to achieve.

WILFRED PETERSON

We began this chapter by realizing that working with attraction is a receptive process. However, you don't leisurely sit back and wait for abundance to just—*poof!*—appear. Yes, indeed, you can change your energetic signature to attract wealth and abundance to you; we covered that in the first few chapters. While magickal attraction is a receptive state, you still need to have the desire and do the work to make the energetic change. This can be achieved by building positive thoughtforms and by working practical magick that is all about attraction, as we did in this chapter as we worked with magnetic sand and lodestones.

However, please remember that when we magnetize ourselves and draw in those changes we want, this is not an idle process. You have to put some effort into it. While that sounds like common sense, you would be surprised…

This always reminds me of folks I have met over the years who get all in a huff and demand to know why their prosperity magick did not work out for them as they envisioned. Why, they have collected many, many books on the subject! (That statement always makes me want to bang my head against the wall.) At that point of the tirade, I typically take a deep breath, put on my most polite smile, and remind the individual that it does not matter how many books you have or how much you read. What matters is that you actually get up, do something about the situation, and then work the magick and cast your spells.

I once had a woman inform me with a great deal of anger that obviously I did not know what I was talking about when it came to spell-crafting, as she had done many different types of prosperity spells and money magick but still could not get a new job.

I cut her off in mid-rant by asking, "Did you enchant your résumé to make it look attractive to prospective employers? Did you email the résumé in during a waxing moon phase or on a Thursday or Sunday for best results? When you went in for an interview, did you carry an herbal charm or work any spells on the day of the interview itself?"

She stumbled to a halt, looked at me, and said, completely straight-faced, "You mean I still have to go and apply for a job, even if I do magick?" She was serious.

And how in the world I kept a straight face when she asked me that, I will never know. Carefully, in a shaky voice, I explained that yes, indeed, magick works best when it is done in partnership with an action on the physical plane—as in filling out applications, sending out résumés, setting up interviews, etc. She walked away a little crestfallen and (I hope) with something to think seriously about.

If you want your prosperity spells to manifest, then you have to be prepared to follow them up with action on the physical realm as well. Manifestation is defined as an outward or perceptible indication, materialization, or visible expression. While materialization is considered to be an occult phenomenon, your prosperity and attraction magick does still require your personal energy and efforts to bring it into manifestation.

This is accomplished in many ways, such as through the law of attraction, where that magickal energy is provided by the fuel of positive thoughtforms. Your desire and wishes for a positive change provide the fuel that your magick needs in order to come to fruition. When you add that fuel to your spellwork, coordinate with the correct astrological and lunar timing, work with complementary deities, and add your physical action on the material plane, this will attract the positive manifestations that you desire. It is a multi-step process, so keep that in mind.

Learning to create prosperity and abundance is a growth process. It does require you to change your thinking and your behavior on both a magickal and a mundane level. At this time, you have changed your energetic signature to a more optimistic one. You are building positive thoughtforms and working actively with the elements in your prosperity and attraction magick, and you are, in fact, becoming magnetic. Now it is even easier to draw in and attract not only wealth but success and healthy abundance.

Chapter Six

Good Luck Charms & Coin Magick

*If one is lucky, a solitary fantasy can totally
transform one million realities.*

MAYA ANGELOU

WHEN NONMAGICKAL FOLKS refer to lucky charms today, they may think of that breakfast cereal that is magically delicious or of the little silver charms worn as clever jewelry. But for Witches and magicians, *charm* has a variety of intriguing meanings.

Classically, the term *charm* is defined as something worn or carried on one's person for its magickal effect. The word *charm* also means (1) to compel with a magickal force, (2) the chanting or singing of a magickal word or verse, or (3) a small ornament worn on a bracelet or chain. Finally, a charm is also identified as an object of magickal power such as an amulet or a talisman.

Back in the old days, people started writing down words of power instead of saying them out loud, with the thought being that a spoken word was fleeting, while a solid object was more enduring. It was then that the term *charm* became associated with physical magickal objects such as stones, shells, or carved animal shapes—what we now think of as magickal amulets and talismans. However, talismans, amulets, and charms are not all the same thing.

To be clear, a talisman is considered to be an object created with a specific magickal goal in mind. It also may be created from any type of material. A goal for a talisman may be increasing personal power or bestowing protection or extra magickal energy upon its wearer. Talismans are also considered to be spiritually significant to their bearer. They are an active and projective type of magick.

An amulet is worn for more general reasons. For example, silver pentagram pendants are most often used as an amulet. A natural amulet may also be made of stone, shell, or wood. Amulets grant protection from harm and ward off negativity and bad luck. According to magickal tradition, an amulet reacts to what is happening in the wearer's world. It does not create any magick specifically. Amulets are passive; they don't project outward, they simply remain and ward your person. It is sort of like a very specific miniature magickal shield.

Charms are intended to bring good luck. They attract success and combine the best qualities of both amulets and talismans in that they may behave in an active magickal manner like a talisman, while they are still generally protective like an amulet. Today, good luck charms are often worn hanging from a necklace as a pendant or grouped together and dangling from a chain to be worn as a necklace or a bracelet. But no matter how they are worn, good luck charms are intended to draw good fortune to their owners.

Wearing good luck charms as jewelry is not a new fad; it is actually an ancient practice. Charms were worn to ward off negative spells, sickness, and injury. The Egyptians wore various trinkets and charms for magickal use, to show their social status, and to connect them to their deities; so, too, did the ancient Greeks and Romans. Medieval knights wore charms for protection into battle, and even in the Dark Ages charms were worn to denote family lineage or the wearer's religious and political beliefs.

Everyone wants to be "lucky," and many cultures throughout time have carried good luck charms with them to attract wealth and good fortune. What sort of charms did they carry? Well, that depends on the culture you look at, but I won't leave you dangling. (Bad charm bracelet pun.)

A Witch's Dozen of Good Luck Charms

I'm sending luck and wishes all wrapped
up in a hug; good things should come
your way with this tiny ladybug.

AUTHOR UNKNOWN

Here is a Witch's dozen (that's thirteen) of traditional magickal good luck charms or amulets and a bit of information about them. You should be able to easily employ these in spells and in the creation of your own personalized good luck charms.

Acorn: The acorn is a symbol of power, vigor, energy, and long-term goals that are manifesting. Consider the old saying that mighty oaks from tiny acorns grow. The acorn is the fruit of the oak tree, and oaks are classically aligned with the planet Jupiter and prosperity magick.

Bee: The honeybee has been a symbol of wealth and good luck since ancient times. If you wear a honeybee emblem, badge, or charm, you are sure to be blessed with good luck. The honeybee is a messenger to the old gods, and the buzzing of bees was thought to be the voice of the Mother Goddess herself.

Bird: The songbird is another traditional good luck charm. Wearing a bird-shaped charm is thought to bring you enthusiasm and cheerful energy for life, which may explain the old saying "happy as a bird" or, if you prefer, "happy as a lark."

Butterfly: The butterfly is symbolic of the manifestation of magick and good luck, as butterflies are not "born"—they transform, or morph, from one creature into another. That fate and energy can be transferred into good fortune. One of my favorite pendants is a silver butterfly with a pentagram in the center. Transformation, luck, manifestation, and magick all rolled into one pretty pendant.

Cat: A cat is considered to be lucky in many magickal cultures. In the United States seeing a white cat is lucky, while in the UK it is a black cat that is considered to be an omen of good fortune. There is also the beckoning cat (*maneki neko*), the lucky cat in Japanese culture. That lucky cat beckons prosperity toward your home or business with a raised paw. There is more information and a spell with *maneki neko* later in the chapter.

Feng Shui Coins: A typical feng shui wealth cure is to tie three feng shui coins together with red ribbon or cord and carry them in your pocket or purse. The coins themselves resemble ancient Chinese coins, which are round with a square hole in the center; this symbolizes the union of heaven and earth. These Chinese feng shui coins work well in prosperity spells of any kind and are nice to have on hand. The most common use of the feng shui coins is for money and protection. The three coins tied together with red cord or ribbon symbolize prosperity, abundance, and good fortune.

Four-Leaf Clover: The clover is a common plant—just take a look in most suburban lawns! However, only one in about ten thousand clovers will have four leaves. But considering the amount of clover in my backyard, I typically do not have problems finding one; it just takes a bit of patience. To find one is to bring good luck. The four-leaf clover symbolizes faith, hope, love, and luck. Some say that the Druids believed when they carried a shamrock that they could see evil spirits approaching. This may explain the plant folklore that carrying a four-leaf clover guards against bad luck and that it offers a bit of magickal protection.

Hamsa (Hand of Fate or Hand of Fatima/Miriam/Venus): This ancient amulet is known in many magickal cultures all over the world. The hamsa is an open right palm, with the palm up and the fingers together and down. This amulet blesses the wearer with good fortune, power, and strength. It also deflects the evil eye. Often the hamsa is embellished with an eye in the palm, a six-pointed star, and beautiful scrollwork on the fingers. If you want to stop negativity, flip your own right hand palm down, fingers up and slightly spread apart. Push the negativity back toward the source while maintaining a strong body posture and say in your mind, "Talk to the hand!"

Horseshoe: A horseshoe nailed upright over the front doorway was thought to bring good luck and prosperity to the entire house-hold. This popular Old World lucky charm is always displayed with the open ends pointing up—that way your luck will never run out. The only time a horseshoe is supposed to be displayed open-end down is over a blacksmith's forge. That way all the good luck would flow onto the forge. You may also place a horseshoe in the northern corner of the home or business in the upright position to reinforce good fortune and positively influence the ambient spiritual energy in the building. Horseshoes are believed to mimic the curves of the crescent moon, so the horseshoe could be used as a subtle moon goddess symbol for the business or home.

Ladybug: Many cultures consider the ladybug auspicious. If a ladybug lands on your hand, it is thought to symbolize good luck and the blessings of the faeries. As ladybugs eat harmful pests such as aphids, their presence in the garden is welcomed by gardeners and farmers alike. Being such a beneficial insect, folks are rather fond of them. Seeing ladybugs in the field was a sign of an especially good harvest. A ladybug with seven spots was thought to be a faery pet, and finding one was especially fortuitous.

Number Seven: Seven is a lucky number in many cultures and magickal traditions. To the ancients, there were seven planets. These visible "planets" were the sun, moon, Mercury, Venus, Mars, Jupiter, and Saturn. The Pythagoreans called seven the perfect number. In Buddhism seven is the number of attaining center. Also, there are the seven seas, and we have seven chakras. There are seven rows, or periods, in the periodic table of elements; seven colors of the rainbow; and, last but not least, seven days of the bewitching week.

Rainbow: Every child knows there is a pot of gold at the end of the rainbow. Not only are rainbows a symbol of hope, they are also a symbol for the Greek messenger goddess Iris. The winged Iris used the rainbow to travel from Olympus to earth and back again. Iris and her rainbow appear in my *Witches Tarot* deck in the Temperance card. If you should see double rainbows, they are supposed to double your luck. And there are seven colors in a rainbow, and seven is a classic lucky number.

Three Skeleton Keys: Three old skeleton-style keys displayed together are an old symbol for health, wealth, and love. Hecate, the queen of the Witches, is associated with three skeleton keys. You could make a clever and subtle magickal necklace or bracelet by using three small charms shaped like keys—check your local arts and crafts store's jewelry-making section.

Silver Charms and the Magick of a Charm Bracelet

I bear a charmed life.

WILLIAM SHAKESPEARE

Just for fun, you may want to take a new look at the practice of charm bracelets. If you have an old silver charm bracelet or a new one, consider adding some good luck or magickal charms to it. If you do have an old charm bracelet that has not seen the light of day for years, get it out, polish it up, and remember what all those charms are for. Add some new magickally themed charms and combine the old charms with the new in a sort of charm bracelet evolution.

If you are intrigued by this idea but do not have a charm bracelet, then there is no time like the present. Any excuse to be crafty is always a good thing, in my opinion. You could create a new magickally themed charm bracelet for yourself. Whether new or old, charm bracelets will always have stories to tell and magick to share.

I became re-fascinated with my charm bracelet after my first book was published. I found my old silver charm bracelet when I was cleaning out my jewelry box about eleven years ago. The last time it had been added to was when my daughter, Erin, was born. In a weird instance of synchronicity, my daughter pounced on my old bracelet and demanded that I explain what all of the silver charms represented. We spent a good half hour while I explained what each charm symbolized, and when and how I had received or bought a charm for myself. As I began to polish up the charms, she quietly asked why I did not have anything witchy on my bracelet. Well, she had me there.

So I set out to "witch up" my own bracelet. It took several years, but that only made the hunt more enjoyable. I found a silver watering can, which I thought would be a fun memento of my having become a

Master Gardener. A friend gifted me with a little silver book charm to represent my first published book, *Garden Witchery*. Then I found a very affordable small silver pentagram the perfect size to add to my bracelet at a flea market one Sunday. Next I bought a funny little charm of a Witch flying on a broom. I scored a 3-D silver Witch hat while in Salem, Massachusetts, at my first author event there. It was even engraved "Salem, Mass." How perfect!

My husband gave me a three-dimensional charm with a cat riding a Witch's broom when my book *The Enchanted Cat* won an award. My daughter found me a silver and black enamel cat charm for my birthday one year, and I found a tiny lighthouse to remember an author event and sightseeing day while in Maine. Recently I found a sterling silver miniature tarot card charm online. I ordered it immediately. It is a tiny silver Rider-Waite version of the Sun card. I happily added it to my charm bracelet to symbolize the release of my *Witches Tarot*.

Whenever I wear that charm bracelet, people ask about the charms. Wearing the bracelet is fun and it always puts me in a good mood. It works…well, like a charm!

A Spell to Empower Your Own Charm Bracelet

Here is a simple spell to enchant your own charm bracelet. No matter what style you have—if your charm bracelet is old and you have recently added to it or if it is new and you have just begun building it—this spell will work out beautifully.

Directions: Hold the charm bracelet in your hands and let the light of the waxing moon shine upon the jewelry. Since silver is a lunar metal, the moonlight is very appropriate. Once the moonlight is shining on the jewelry, repeat the following spell verse:

> *Silver charms show my personal history*
> *For love and luck, I now empower this jewelry.*

These ornaments and trinkets jingle and jangle
The spell they cast is anything but newfangled.
By all the power of three times three
I now enchant this charming jewelry.

Now slip on that bracelet and enjoy the magick and good luck that follows.

Maneki Neko
The Beckoning Good Luck Cat

By associating with the cat one
only risks becoming richer.

SIDONIE-GABRIELLE COLETTE

The "beckoning cat" is a familiar image in Japanese culture. Today it is one of the most popular amulets for good luck and drawing prosperity in the world. Sometimes called a lucky cat, money cat, or fortune cat, the beckoning cat figurine gained popularity in Japan in the 1870s; the first mention of it in print was in a Japanese newspaper in 1876. The Japanese name for the beckoning cat is *maneki neko* (pronounced MA-neck-ee-NECK-o).

This lucky cat brings good fortune to its owner. Typically it's a ceramic figurine and it has a familiar gesture: one paw up, pads out, as if it is beckoning to you. In the Japanese culture, the beckoning motion is made by holding the hand up, palm out, and then folding the fingers up and down.

You may see different variations of *maneki neko*. If his left paw is raised, then he is thought to bring in customers. If his right paw is raised in the beckoning motion, then the cat figurine is for good luck and wealth. There is another school of thought that says a raised left paw attracts money, while a raised right paw protects it. And if both paws are raised, it is protective for both the home and the business.

Place the figurine in the window looking out and it will beckon good fortune inside. Or you may keep it inside your home or on the counter at your place of business. Just make sure *maneki neko* is positioned across from the front main entrance. Some of these figurines have a slot in the back of them like a piggy bank. If yours does, then feed it a few coins to get the prosperity magick started. Finally, legend says you must make a four-year commitment when you work with *maneki neko*, so keep that in mind.

Magickal Colors of Maneki Neko

There are many different versions of *maneki neko*, which comes in lots of colors and poses. Here are some of the colors you will find and their meanings:

- if the beckoning cat is wearing a bib and bell, this symbolizes wealth and material abundance
- tri-colored or calico (classic and the most popular) is thought to be the luckiest of all
- white means purity and good things coming your way
- gold is for wealth and prosperity
- red or pink is for love and relationships
- green symbolizes good health, education, and victory
- black wards off evil spirits and stalkers and is protective

Empowering Your Cat Figurine

Here is a practical magick spell for empowering your *maneki neko* figurine. I would work this spell during a waxing moon (as the moon increases, so too shall your fortune) or, at the very least, work this on a Sunday (the sun's day for success) or a Thursday (Jupiter's day for prosperity). Hold the figurine up and allow either moonlight or sunlight to shine upon it and empower it. Visualize the many ways prosperity will come to your door. Build those positive thoughtforms, and allow the law of attraction to give this a bit more oomph. Then repeat the following spell verse with intention:

Maneki neko, sweet little beckoning cat
Now attract abundance to me just like that.
With your cheerful colors and vibrant energy
And your paw raised high, you draw in prosperity.
A joyful good luck talisman, you do brighten up my days
Attracting good fortune to me in many magickal ways.

Your *maneki neko* figurine is now empowered, enchanted, and ready to go. Be sure to place it in a window facing out to draw prosperity in the door, or place it on your business's counter cheerfully facing the front door so it draws more customers in.

Lucky Cat Candle Spell

As long as we are on the subject of lucky cats, the Egyptian cat goddess Bast or Bastet is purr-fect to work with for prosperity spells, as she was a luxurious deity associated with pleasure and fertility. If you cannot locate a cat-shaped candle at your local metaphysical store, look online or keep an eye out around August through October for novelty Halloween candles shaped like black cats. When you find them, stock up.

Also, if you have a feline familiar in your home, be sure to keep this spell well out of a curious kitty's reach. There is something about Bast spells that draws cats just like a magnet, so be warned.

Timing: Friday, associated with Venus and love
    and complementary to Bast

Moon Phase: waxing or full

Supplies:

- black cat-shaped candle
- a fireproof saucer or plate (to place the candle and sand on)
- magnetic sand
- 3 tumbled tiger's-eye stones
- a lighter or matches
- a safe, flat surface to set up the candle spell on, or place the whole business inside of a large metal cauldron to keep it safe from curious cats or small children (I put these sorts of spells inside the cauldron and then place the cauldron up and on top of our wood-burning stove)

Directions: Hold the cat-shaped candle in your hands and bless the spell candle with the following lines:

> As I hold this black cat-shaped spell candle in my hands
> I enchant it to send good fortune across the land.
> Now burn with purpose both bright and true
> May I be blessed in all that I do.

Now place the cat-shaped candle on the fireproof saucer. Surround the candle with a thin ring of magnetic sand, then wipe your hands clean. Add the tiger's-eye tumbled stones on the work surface/bottom of the cauldron around the *outside* edges of the saucer.

Take a few moments to ground and center yourself. Imagine all of the wonderful and positive ways your good fortune will manifest. Build those positive thoughtforms, and allow the law of attraction to give this a bit more oomph. Then repeat the following spell verse with intention as you light the candle:

> Little cat-shaped spell candle created in deepest black
> Draw good fortune to me and claw negativity back.

Add some tiger's-eye stones for wealth and for protection true
While magnetic sand attracts success in all that I do.
With Bast's blessing this spell now manifests in many charming ways
Bringing joy and wealth into my life that will last all of my days.

Allow the cat-shaped candle to burn out in a safe place. Be sure to keep an eye on it. Once it has burned down, pocket the tiger's-eye stones and keep them with you for good luck, protection, and prosperity. I would break up any leftover melted wax and sand into small chunks and use in future charm bags for prosperity and good luck.

Coins in Ancient Rome

Silver and gold are not the only coin;
virtue too passes current all over the world.

EURIPIDES

There are three main civilizations from where coins developed: Greek, Indian, and Chinese. The Chinese coin is the most unchanged through history, while the Greek coin has gone through many incarnations and was the direct ancestor of the Roman coin.

The patron goddess of the Roman mint was Juno Moneta. She is one of the many faces of the mother goddess Juno. Juno was the supreme mother deity in Rome; among her many titles was the most important, Juno Regina, or Juno the Queen. It is from her name that the month of June takes its title, and interestingly enough it is still one of the most auspicious months to marry in.

Juno Moneta ruled over several activities of state, including the issuing of money. In 269 BCE Rome introduced a new silver coin, the denarius, which was created in Juno Moneta's very own temple. The coin showed the image of the goddess and also her surname, Moneta. Other versions of Juno's coins depicted Juno reclining, holding a cornucopia or scales with money piled at her feet, or with a peacock at her side. The frequent melting and reissuing of coins kept the mints at the temple of Juno Moneta in constant operation for four hundred years. Apparently there was a "constant stream" of coinage being produced.

It is interesting to note that the Latin word *currere*, which means "to run" or "to flow," is where the modern word *currency* originated from. The goddess's name Moneta eventually came to refer to the place where the coins were made (the mint) and its product (money). Juno Moneta's ancient temple was found on the Capitoline Hill. Today, the site of the temple of Juno Moneta is under the foundation of a modern brick church in Rome called Santa Maria in Aracoeli.

Coin and Metal Magick

May your pockets be heavy and your heart be light.
May good luck pursue you each morning and night.

IRISH BLESSING

In the previous chapter there were a few spells that worked with magnetic sand and coins, but working with a lucky coin is a bit different. A lucky coin can fall under the category of a "good luck charm" or a talisman, depending on what you choose to do with it. When it comes to coin magick, like attracts like. A lucky coin may be a rare coin, one minted in your birth year, or just a cool old coin you found on your travels.

With coin magick, you are using the coins to attract or "draw in" even more money and wealth. Coins are actually preferable to paper money for prosperity spells as they are easier to handle and do not burn, tear, or crumple. Coin magick revolves around metal magick. The metals of copper, silver, and gold have their own magickal qualities, so consider these as you begin to work with various coins in spells found in this book or in spells of your own design.

Copper: Copper is thought to quickly attract whatever it is you most desire, which makes sense when you consider that its astrological association is the planet Venus. Copper is a receptive metal that is classically used to draw money, and it is also associated with the element of water. Copper is a conductor of electricity and is considered to be a lucky metal. Not surprisingly, copper magickal jewelry is making a comeback these days. Copper is complementary to any spells relating to your career as well. Look for pennies minted before the year 1982—those have more copper in them—or scout around for the wheat penny. These were minted in the years 1909–1958 and have the two ears of wheat on the back of the coin and would be complementary to the prosperity and good fortune goddesses Juno Moneta, Pax, Abuntania, and Fortuna.

Silver: Silver dimes are a classic in American folk magick—especially the Mercury dime. Silver has the astrological association of the moon and the element of water, and it is considered to be a feminine, receptive metal. Use that receptive power to "draw in" prosperity, good fortune, and success. The Mercury dime has a high silver content compared to today's dimes. This dime was minted between the years 1916 and 1945. This particular dime shows a picture of Liberty wearing a winged cap. However, folks became confused by the image and said it looked like the old Roman god Mercury, and the name stuck. The Mercury dime is a gambler's charm (not surprising when you stop to consider that the god Mercury was a patron of gamblers), and this coin is a classic accoutrement in prosperity magick of all kinds.

Gold: The most valuable of metals—it is what our currency is based on—gold is preferred in traditional coin magick. You can always be practical and work with gold jewelry if you don't want to invest in gold coins. Gold is associated with the sun and the element of fire. This metal is considered to have masculine energies and possesses a projective, active type of energy. Gold has naturally been linked with deity throughout time. Gold promotes wisdom and is thought to boost your personal power and help you learn to harness your magick and direct it with less effort. Gold sun-shaped talismans designed for success and wealth magick would be especially projective and potent. Also, if you habitually only wear silver jewelry, consider balancing it out with a little gold. That way your receptive and projective energies will be in harmony.

ℌ Little Practical Advice…

Sometimes it is the simplest, seemingly most inane,
most practical stuff that matters the most to someone.

PATTY DUKE

When it comes to finding copper, silver, and gold coins for your spells, you may need to be creative and think outside the box. If you work in retail you will probably come across old pennies and dimes—the silver dimes especially as they make a different "clink" when they hit the cash register drawer. Now, I don't know about you, but I don't have gold coins just lying about.

I did, however, take a little trip to the local coin shop, but I balked at dropping twenty bucks for a gold coin. I did pick up a couple of worn silver Mercury dimes for a few bucks, though. If you do want to work with gold coins but need to watch your budget, consider this practical alternative: use the golden dollar coin instead, specifically the Sacagawea coin.

The dollar coin that portrays Sacagawea was released into circulation in January 2000. It is a golden-colored coin that is copper bonded to layers of manganese brass. So while it is technically *not* gold, it has a golden color, its center is copper, and it portrays a brave, adventurous young woman carrying her infant son on her back. Sacagawea, in case you have lived under a rock, was the Native American guide who led Lewis and

Clark on their expedition across the west. I like the idea of using a coin that portrays a strong, capable young mother—hello, goddess energy—and I have to tell you the Sacagawea coins work beautifully in any spells I have incorporated them into, so give them a try for yourself.

A Pocket Spell

Another fun bit of folk magick to try with old silver coins is to take three silver coins and flip them to gain prosperity. Legend says to line up the trio of silver coins, heads up, under the light of a full moon one hour before midnight. A windowsill would be ideal for this. After midnight, flip the three silver coins over to tails up for one hour. Then pocket the lunar-charged coins and attract more prosperity straight to your wallet.

Try this short little spell verse to go with it. Say this after the last hour is over and you are putting the coins in your pocket or wallet.

> *Under the lovely silver moon so bright*
> *I enchant this trio of dimes tonight.*
> *With all the power of three times three*
> *These coins will draw in prosperity.*

Mercury Dime Spell for Mercury Retrograde

To close up this chapter, here is a coin spell that will help to minimize the effects Mercury retrograde can cause. It's a simple spell and one that is fun to do.

When Mercury is in retrograde, it appears as if the planet is moving backwards in the sky. Typically this happen three times within the calendar year. For a little over three weeks, you can expect communication snafus, a bit of bad luck, email problems, computer issues, travel arrangements, and electronic appliances to go a little wonky.

Think of Mercury retrogrades like a gigantic hill that you have to climb. For the first week, problems really start to rise up; it seems hard, and it feels like you will never see the top of the hill. Then, in the second week, things hold steady; you reach the crest of the hill. Things start to level out, but you are tired and aggravated, with continuing minor aggravations. By the third week, we start to slide down the back of the hill, the journey becomes easier, and problems will begin to taper off.

Another (more positive) way to think of Mercury retrogrades is that it is time to rethink, reconsider, and reevaluate where you are standing. Stop and reassess how you intend to move forward with your goals. (Notice all of the "re's" in there? The word *retrograde* starts with re-, so look at other words with a "re" in front of them.)

Now take a deep breath and relax. Mercury retrogrades can be challenging, but they do not have to be a dramafest. They are what they are, so brace yourself, reexamine your reactions, move forward with a positive attitude, and tackle those challenges!

Supplies

- a gray votive candle
- a straight pin or boline (something to carve the Mercury retrograde symbols in the candle: ☿ ℞)
- a silver Mercury dime (check your local coin store)
- a votive cup
- a lighter or matches
- a safe, flat surface

Directions: Acquire a Mercury dime and a gray votive candle. We use the color gray in this spell as it symbolizes neutrality. Next, engrave the astrological symbols of Mercury in retrograde on the side of the candle, then draw a large X over the top of the symbols. Lastly, draw a circle around the entire crossed-out Mercury retrograde symbols so the symbol will be crossed out *and* encircled.

Now hold the unlit candle in your hands. Empower the spell candle and say:

As I hold this neutralizing spell candle in my hands
It will nullify retrograde's effect across my own land.
Now burn with purpose both bright and true
May I be blessed in all that I do.

Set the Mercury dime next to the candleholder. Put the votive candle in the candleholder and light it. Remember that votive candles turn to liquid—you have to use a candleholder unless you want a big puddle of wax on your altar. Once the candle is lit, take a deep, calming breath and ground and center. Then repeat the invocation three times:

Mercury, trickster god of cunning,
speed, travel, and communication,
Hear my call today and help me travel through
this time easily and with no harm.
With this coin and candle spell I neutralize
the effects of Mercury in retrograde.
Any retrograde problems, annoyances, difficulties,
and snafus will now begin to fade.

Close up the spell with these lines:

By all the power of three times three
This spell will turn out successfully.

Allow the candle to burn in a safe place until it goes out on its own. Save the Mercury dime and reuse it in other coin spells that call for a silver coin.

Witch Tip: Work this spell as often as you need to during the retrograde. I always find that working this on a Wednesday—the day devoted to the god Mercury—increases its effectiveness. Blessed be!

Chapter Seven

REMOVING OBSTACLES
TO YOUR SUCCESS

Obstacles cannot crush me. Every obstacle
yields to stern resolve. He who is fixed to
a star does not change his mind.

LEONARDO DA VINCI

I AM ABOUT to open this chapter with some really eloquent verbiage. Here you are, bouncing along, all proud of your new prosperity goals and successes and the progress you have made, and then all of a sudden—*whap!* You get hit with some major expense you had not planned on. Were you cursed? Did some jealous Witch zap you with a hex because you were doing well and they were not? Did your spells stop working? Did you get complacent?

Maybe or maybe not. Sometimes—and here comes that aforementioned eloquent verbiage—shit just happens.

This can happen to anyone. A trip to the emergency room, a car repair, your normally sensible kid calling from college to announce they screwed up their student checking account and are broke… Unexpected bills hit, and we have to deal with them. Life loves to throw little challenges our way. The trick is *not* to let yourself get dragged down. You have to keep on working your magick and building those positive thoughtforms. Sure, setbacks and roadblocks can be upsetting, but take a breath, consider all of the resources at your disposal, and get to work!

For example, while I was finishing up this book, our heater gave up the ghost. Honestly, the heating and air conditioning system was over thirty years old, and we had planned to get a new system in the spring, after I got my royalty check. But you know what they say about the best-laid plans...

So on New Year's Day, the heater up and died. The hubs tooled around with it and it sort of ran again, but the house was very cold. Who was I kidding? For years in the house it had been chilly every winter and blazing hot every summer. Our energy bills were very high, and we knew it was from the old furnace and a/c unit. We had realized that the old unit was inefficient but were hanging in there to put a large down payment and then finance the rest in April. Obviously that's not the way it all worked out.

So on January 2 we called in a repairman and got the bad news. He showed us that there were burn marks and smoke stains inside the heater where the elements had caught fire and burnt out. That was sobering.

Also, our system was so old that the manufacturer had gone out of business and the company that made replacement parts was also closed. (Not surprising; during the last repair several years prior, it had taken weeks to find new parts.) So we sat down and looked at our options. We were able to finance it, and—holy gods—it was not much different from buying a car.

As we were considered an emergency situation, the very next morning they showed up with a team of guys and ripped out the old system and installed the new energy-efficient one. It took all day, so I built a fire in the woodstove, snuggled in with a friend's book that I had promised to read and give a blurb for, and stayed out of the way. The crew was polite, neat, and worked quickly. They left eight hours later, dropping off cards and telling us to let them know if we had any questions at all, and they would come right back.

For the first week, we tried to get used to the fancy new digital thermostat and all of the noises the new system made. Wow, amazing what a new energy-efficient system can do! I started to turn down the temperature on the thermostat right away. What a novel idea: the heater comes on, and it gets warm. Ha.

Then I began to notice every time the heater's compression unit kicked on, it was very loud outside and our lights in the house dimmed. After watching that for a week, I called the company back. They sent out a guy who double-checked everything—yes, we had plenty of power to run the unit; in fact, it pulled less power than the old unit. He then ordered a compression blanket, which is basically a muffler for the outdoor unit so when the compressor kicked on it would be quieter. That was covered by the install and so forth. They would be happy to add that free of charge, as a courtesy.

Then he suggested we add an extra item to the unit that would not be covered under the install. Designed for much larger units, it would take a bit of the pressure off the main power. However, because it was technically not needed, it would not be covered. And no, it was not cheap. I told him I'd think about it, and he promised that someone would be back to install the blanket thingy (technical term) within a few days.

A few days later, yet another guy from the company came in. I was knee-deep in writing but set it aside, as he was in and out of the house and my cat had decided to take a shine to him. Brie, my normally shy little calico, kept trying to climb in his lap while he worked and retested the new system.

My goodness, the guy did not stop talking. He cheerfully informed me he had been married four times and was getting ready for his fourth divorce and all about his kids, his cats, and so forth. Good god. Happy as a clam, he sat on the laundry room floor and talked. Nonstop. He too suggested that we add the extra switch thing to the unit, and I declined that offer. It was simply too expensive.

Back and forth, he went inside and outside, and once he came back in to get his tools and leave, he leaned against the wall and proceeded to cheerfully ask me questions about what it was like to be a writer.

Ten more minutes went by…I tried to steer him toward the door.

Twenty minutes went by…I announced that I had to get back to work and thanks for everything.

Then I pulled out my ace in the hole—the one thing guaranteed to have him scampering out of the house. When he stopped to ask what sort of books I wrote (my standard answer is "New Age nonfiction"), instead I said, with a calculated smile, "I write books on Witchcraft."

There. Done. Now he would go.

His eyes lit up and—crap, did that backfire.

Ohmygod, he announced breathlessly. *How cool.* Could I tell him if his father who had passed away was okay in the afterlife? Amazed at having my "master plan" turn and bite me in the ass, I told him what his father's first name was. I did not ask, I announced it. He looked at me wide-eyed, as I had nailed it and there was no way I could have known. So I answered him that yes, his father was fine.

And what about his current girlfriend? he inquired, all wide-eyed. In frustration, I heard myself ask who the woman was in his life whose name ended with an A, as she would be a good fit for him. Apparently his new girlfriend was Lisa or Linda—honestly, I can't remember. Another ten minutes passed before I could get him out the front door and onto the porch, where he continued to cheerfully chatter.

Now, he never made me uncomfortable. I was just trying to be polite and he was so damn cheerful it was hard to get angry, but I was frustrated and teetering toward annoyance. Finally my phone rang. I picked it up and told him it was my editor (it was a friend), he waved, and finally, he left.

A few minutes later, he was outside banging around on the outdoor unit. Well, hell. What was he doing now? At that point I was very tempted to call his company and complain about his behavior, when he came back to the front door and announced that he had gone ahead and installed the extra expensive switch anyway and that he wouldn't charge us for it.

He came inside, tested it out, and everything worked out fine. No more dimming lights. So once again I ushered him to the door…ten more minutes passed. This guy made *me* look shy and retiring, I have to say. And finally he left for good.

The point of the story? I am so glad you asked. I got the extra switch thingy for free. I saved about three hundred dollars because I was pleasant, listened, reassured him that his father was okay in the afterlife, and confirmed that his new girlfriend was a wonderful lady. So magick happened and I did not even plan it. Nice.

My husband, who works the night shift, had slept through the repairman's visit. When he woke up later that afternoon, he laughed until he cried when I told him about the chatty repairman.

"You pulled out both the I *am a Witch* card and yanked stuff out of his head, and that *still* didn't scare him into leaving?"

"No," I said in disgust. "It only made him more talkative."

My husband chuckled, said it was handy to have a Witch for a wife, and went to check for himself how the heater worked with the new switch.

As for myself, I had a glass of wine at three in the afternoon and felt decadent. Then after my husband left for work, I finally was able to get back to my writing.

So see, my life isn't perfect either. I do not live in a mansion on a hill, more like a ranch-style house in the 'burbs. Anyway, I roll with the challenges life throws at me. I use magick to smooth the way when necessary and do the best I can.

And so should you.

Personal Magickal Energy:
Troubleshooting Prosperity Spells

Working hard and working smart
sometimes can be two different things.

BYRON DORGAN

If you seem to be encountering resistance to the prosperity spells you cast, then you need to look at this from a whole new perspective. It may be time to do some magickal troubleshooting and diagnose where the problem began and how best to unravel it. Remember that the speed and style in which your prosperity magick unfolds is the direct result of your intention and your emotional focus at the time you cast that spell.

This all comes together to equal the amount of what I call Personal Magickal Energy, or PME for short. This PME total represents the amount of thought, effort, style, and power that you put into the stalled prosperity spell when you first cast it. If you add those factors all up, you would give yourself a PME number. Case in point: try to rate that stalled prosperity spell's performance on a scale from one to ten. This is simple to do and it can be very, very illuminating as to why your spellwork stalled or was blocked from a successful manifestation.

Here is an example. We will say that a ten on the PME scale represents your magickal best, as in absolute perfection. You brought your A game and pulled out all the stops. Everything was the best you could possibly make it—as in the spell's astrological timing, your magickal accoutrements, a correct emotional state, keeping the Hermetic principles in mind, and so forth.

Or were you honestly more at the low end of the PME scale, as in a one, meaning that you just went through the motions? Did you half-ass the magick? I know that sounds a little irreverent, but seriously…did you? If you just rattled off a spell you found in some book and maybe lit a green candle for effect, with no thought of correct emotional states, astrological timing, and so forth…well, that's going to rate as a very low

Personal Magickal Energy number. Here is something vitally important for you to wrap your mind around: a low energetic effort equals a low magickal reward.

Keeping all this in mind, now try to figure out where you were on that energetic scale in regards to that stalled prosperity spell, and then ascribe it an honest number on that PME scale from one to ten. The higher the number, the better you believe your magickal performance and energy sent out to manifest a change was.

So, for the sake of argument, we will say that you gave yourself a five on the PME scale. You did the best you could and worked in a waxing moon phase for increase. But maybe that was on a Saturday, come to think of it…Saturdays are best for binding, banishing, and minimizing negativity. Well, damn. Maybe that prosperity spell wasn't as potent or powerful as you'd first imagined it to be…

Now consider how much energetic resistance from the mundane world you may have been working against. Give that energetic resistance a number from one to ten as well. Here are a few more real-life examples to give you a clearer idea of how to rate the resistance you have encountered.

Was all hell breaking loose? If collection agencies are calling or you just got laid off, that would be a ten. Let's say your hours got cut or they stopped overtime that you counted on to pay the bills; then I'd put that energetic resistance at around a seven. You've still got a job but things aren't looking so rosy.

On the other hand, if things were just getting tight with the budget or an unexpected bill hit and you figured you'd better start working the prosperity magick before things got too grim, then I'd give that situation about a four. Now subtract that energetic resistance number from your PME score, and look at the total number. There may be your problem.

So let's say you rated your spell's PME at a five, meaning you did the best you could but honestly there could have been some improvement. The energetic resistance was that they cut your hours at work, which would rate a seven. So that gives you a whopping total of a negative two.

Well, hello there. You just found your problem. There is more resistance to your spell than you invested energetically.

Getting your hours cut at work is serious, and a spell that you honestly rate at a five on the PME scale is not going to be of much assistance. Just like many things in our world, you do get out of your magick whatever you put into it.

Also, this would be the perfect opportunity to point out that being angry about your current financial situation, panicking, or just feeling hopeless can and will smother any type of positive spellwork that you do. Give yourself some time to plot and plan your prosperity magick for the best possible results—maybe even take a day or two to make sure you are in a correct energetic state. Being too impatient to work this type of magick correctly or just tossing magick around because you panicked may cause unexpected and even chaotic results.

So let's take a look at some common magickal snafus or mistakes that can affect your Personal Magickal Energy and the correct manifestation of your prosperity magick.

Solving Common Magickal Snafus

*You have to learn the rules of the game. And
then you have to play better than anyone else.*

ALBERT EINSTEIN

Error, mistake, blunder, slip-up, gaffe, screw-up, bungle, mishap… no matter what you call it, a magickal snafu is a chance to learn and improve. This as an opportunity for a magickal epiphany. The best way to learn something is to look at your past magickal actions and see if there is room for improvement. We all make mistakes with our magick, and the difference between an advanced—or, as I prefer to call them, adept—practitioner is that they learn from their past errors, and then grow and advance.

Adept practitioners embrace *any* opportunity for the chance to improve. This is not where you should feel bad about your spellcasting performance; this is where you troubleshoot and learn so you can improve. I am not trying to tear you down. I want to empower you and teach you something new. Put your game face on. Be confident and bold! Look at this as a chance to gather more knowledge and information.

- The first thing I would double-check would be to see if Mercury was retrograde when you cast your spell. That can cause many problems with how your prosperity spell ultimately manifests. Refer to chapter 6 for more information, and take another look at the Mercury Dime Spell for Mercury Retrograde in chapter 6.

- Did you work *with* the Hermetic principles and law of attraction or against them? Not sure? Well, there's no time like the present. Take another look at those principles and the LOA in chapter 1 and see how you can correctly apply them to your next prosperity spell. You need to learn that information cold.

- How did you word your spell exactly? Did you write down your spell verse or did you just off-the-cuff ask for something nonspecific? Be careful what you ask for. Being specific and cautious with both *what* and *how* you say your spells during the performance of magick is vitally important. Take another look at chapter 3 and see what you can improve when it comes to the mechanics of your spellwork.

- Last but not least, what sort of emotional state were you in when you cast? I have been harping on that point for a good reason. Your personal magickal energy should always be optimistic and focused on positive abundance and creating more wealth. It should not be centered on money worries or fears of lack and poverty. Be aware of and responsible for what you create with your energetic thoughtforms.

The list below is an at-a-glance correspondence chart of the most opportune correspondences for your prosperity magick.

Correspondences for Prosperity Magick

Most Opportune Moon Phase: waxing moon (new to full)

Most Opportune Associated Planets: sun, Jupiter

Most Opportune Days of the Week: Sunday (sun's day) for success, Thursday (Jupiter's day) for prosperity and abundance

Most Opportune Colors for Prosperity Magick: gold (for the sun and success), green (for all general prosperity work), royal blue or purple (Jupiter's colors)

Complementary Tarot Cards: the Magician, the Emperor, the Wheel of the Year/Wheel of Fortune, the Sun, Ace of Pentacles, and also the Nine and Ten of Pentacles; work with these as props in spells for good luck, increase, abundance, a prosperous family, and a happy home

Complementary Accoutrements: golden magnetic sand, lodestones

Complementary Crystals: aventurine, bloodstone, chrysoprase, citrine, emerald, jade, tourmaline, lepidolite, malachite, moss agate, rhodochrosite, tiger's-eye, turquoise

Complementary Herbs: bay, cinquefoil, clover, dandelion, High John the Conqueror root, hollyhock, honeysuckle, mint, money plant, oak, pine, shamrock, sunflower

Complementary Deities: Abuntania, Lakshmi, Yemaya, Juno Moneta, Fortuna, Tyche, Ganesha

Ganesha:
The Remover of Obstacles

I meant what I said and I said what I meant.
An elephant's faithful one hundred percent.

DR. SEUSS

Ganesha, or Ganesh, is the pot-bellied, much-beloved elephant-headed Hindu god known as the remover of obstacles. Associated with success and prosperity, he is a popular god in the Hindu pantheon. Ganesha is traditionally a very popular deity with merchants and traders, and he is recognizable to just about everyone, which explains why he is thought to be the god for every man.

He is also a destroyer of evil as well as a god of education, scholarships, wisdom, and a happy home life. As was mentioned previously, he is associated with Lakshmi. It is said that wherever there is success and prosperity, there is Ganesha. Ganesha is all loving, and anyone may successfully work with him. If you are facing obstacles, whether spiritual or material, Ganesha is happy to help. This elephant-headed deity personifies the primal sound of OM. His large elephant ears mean he is always ready to listen to your prayers and requests.

In classic iconography, Ganesha is portrayed with four arms and one tusk. Legend says he broke off one of his tusks to write an important Indian epic. There is also a mouse at his feet. The mouse is considered to be his "vehicle," as the mouse is quick and able to get into the tiniest of places—just like Ganesha's magick.

If you are facing spiritual or material obstacles, need help obtaining a scholarship or grant (for yourself or a child), or applying for school or a job, then Ganesha is the deity to call upon.

As I worked on this chapter, my daughter was applying to graduate schools, as she planned to get her master's degree in museum sciences. While she filled out all of the applications to the various universities, she commented that she could use a little luck or some divine intervention. I mentioned what I was working on, and she liked that idea. So I decided to test this out and worked the following spell to Ganesha.

A week later, her first choice for graduate school sent her a letter; she was not accepted to the program, and she was devastated. I will admit, I wondered about that. Instinctively I felt that the magick was still in play, so I kept quiet and supported her as she adjusted her plans and then thought about other options. Three days after her disappointment, I got a phone call from her in the late afternoon.

"Mom...," she began in a very shaky voice.

"Are you hurt?" I interrupted. I could tell she was upset, and I knew she was on her way home from work, so I imagined a car accident.

"I'm fine," she said softly, her voice still shaking.

"What's happened?" I asked, still very concerned.

"I got accepted into graduate school," she said, her voice wobbling. Then she proceeded to tell me it was closer to home than the other university she had applied to and was much more affordable.

"That's fantastic!" I congratulated her.

"I already spoke to the dean of my department. Mom, I am really going!" she said excitedly.

At the moment, she is knee-deep in filling out paperwork and getting her finances and loans in order. After looking at the second university, I actually think it will be a better fit for her. Of course, her father and I, and her boyfriend, all like that it's only about four hours away. Sometimes things do work better than expected when you sit back and let the magick manifest. So thanks, Ganesha. Big guy, you came through in a spectacular fashion!

For best results, spells requesting Ganesha's assistance are best worked in the waxing moon phase (for increase).

Removing Obstacles with Ganesha Spell

Here is a pretty spell that calls on Ganesha. You will notice that it allows for some personalization in the fifth line.

Timing: waxing moon phase

Day of the Week: Thursday (for general prosperity), Wednesday (best for communication magick and for spells involving scholarships, grants, or to help with applications to a university)

Supplies and Directions: Traditionally, fresh red flowers and sweets called *ladoo* are left as offerings to him. A little cookie or a wrapped hard candy in yellow or red would work out nicely too. Suggested candle colors for Ganesha are red and yellow. Any sweet-smelling incense would be a lovely addition. For an affordable fresh flower option, go to the local florist and pick up a few stems of red mini carnations. These little flowers smell terrific and last a long time.

I also suggest printing out a little picture of Ganesha and adding it to your workspace. You could glue the image onto a plain red or yellow jar candle if you like. If you prefer to just have the picture sitting there, then put it in a central place of honor.

Take a few moments and set this spell up respectfully. Set up your altar as nicely as you can, arranging the work area with love and care. Be sure to put yourself in the proper mood and energetic place. Remember that PME information from earlier and act accordingly and with intention.

When you are ready to begin, empower and bless your red and yellow spell candles to Ganesha with the following verse:

> *As I hold these spell candles in my hands*
> *They represent the help of the god of every man.*
> *Now brightly burn with purpose both strong and true*
> *Obstacles will be removed from what I do.*

After the candles have been empowered, you may light them. If you are adding incense, then get that working as well.

Reverently arrange the fresh flowers and the sweets. When you are ready, say the following verse:

OM Ganesha, OM Ganesha, OM Ganesha
The loving elephant-headed god of every man.
Hear my heartfelt request for your assistance
I ask that you gently remove any obstacle that blocks my success.
Make the path to [prosperity/the scholarship/the grant] clear for me
I offer you these flowers and sweets with thanks, respect, and love.
By the elements of earth, air, fire, and water
Grant the requests of your sons and daughters.

Allow the candles to burn in a safe place until they go out on their own. Place the fresh flowers in a vase and keep them in a prominent place. Place the cookie and (unwrapped) candy outdoors in the garden, and allow nature to reclaim them. When the flowers fade, add them to your yard waste to be recycled or to your compost pile.

May Ganesha clear the way for you with the most wondrous of success!

The Tower Card Spell to Remove Blocks and Energetic Resistance

Here is a dramatic spell that works with the energies of the waning moon and the Tower card from your tarot deck. This time we work with the waning moon because we want obstacles and resistance to your previous prosperity work to decrease, wane, and disappear. This is the magick of working during the waning moon phase.

In my *Witches Tarot* deck, the Tower card shows stormy, dark skies surrounding a tower that sits high on a cliff. Lightning snakes down from storm clouds and strikes the tower, knocking a crown off the top.

The Tower card from Witches Tarot

Within the tower a fire burns, which cleanses and transforms. Two figures fall from the tower—they are tumbling out headfirst. This illustrates that this event is completely out of their control.

The tower depicted in this major arcana card symbolizes our ambitions. The ruby-studded crown represents the ego; in magickal traditions, rubies are used to intensify awareness. The lightning bolt in this scene represents that there is now a flash of insight; the bright light of truth will illuminate any questionable situation. Blocks are being removed and negative energy is finally being broken through. Transformation is occurring; reevaluation is necessary at this time.

When the card turns up in a reading, it means that there will be a shocking revelation or an event that forever changes the way you see yourself and the people around you. This is not necessarily a negative thing. Now that all of that built-up pressure has been released from the tower, the fire inside will both cleanse and transform it. What spiritual blocks or obstacles you once faced are now removed. What you learn will end up being helpful in the long run.

Using the Tower card's powerful imagery in your spellwork reinforces that the obstacles you face and resistance you are working against will be eliminated. Not only will they be removed, they also will be transformed into something more positive.

Timing
- Work this particular tarot spell during the waning moon (from the day after the full moon until the night before the new moon).
- Work this spell at sunset on a Saturday (Saturn's day). This is very important. Check your astrological calendar and time it correctly. Put some effort into this and raise up that PME score! This specific lunar phase, day of the week, and time of day will help to banish those obstacles and remove resistance. Consider

that this is the close of the week and the end of the daylight hours; that is a powerful combination for removing obstacles and problems.

Supplies and Directions

- a black candle (to remove obstacles)—votive or taper—and a coordinating candleholder
- the Tower card from your tarot deck
- a lighter or matches
- a safe, flat work surface where the candle can safely burn until it goes out on its own

Be sure to put yourself in the proper mood and energetic place. Remember that PME information from earlier, and act accordingly and with intention.

Timing is crucial for this spell. Lay out the card in the center of your altar or work space. Arrange the black candle in its holder just behind the card. Place your hands on either side of the candle in the holder, and empower it with the following lines:

> As I *surround this black spell candle with my hands*
> I *empower it to send magick across the land.*
> *Now burn with purpose both bright and true*
> *May I be blessed in all that I do.*

Take a few moments and look carefully at the imagery in the Tower card. Visualize any spiritual obstacles or spell resistance that you may have faced now being safely nullified and removed. Keep your thoughtforms both positive and confident.

Light the candle and repeat the following spell verse:

Like a bolt of lightning straight out of a storm's heart
Any resistance to my work must now depart.
All obstacles are removed, the way forward is now clear
Prosperity comes freely to me from both far and near.
For the good of all, with harm to none
By tarot's magick, this spell is done!

Leave the card in place for as long as the candle burns, making sure to keep an eye on the candle. Then, when the candle is spent, return the card to your tarot deck. Blessed be.

Tough Times Call for Creative Magick

Success is not measured by what you accomplish
but by the opposition you have encountered and
the courage with which you have maintained
the struggle against overwhelming odds.

ORISON SWETT MARDEN

When obstacles happen and put roadblocks in the path of your success or you encounter resistance to your cast spells, you need to hang tough and keep working. The last two spells in this chapter will help you do just that! Come on, pull yourself up by your witchy black bootlaces. No moping is allowed. Get back up, dust your magickal self off, and start working your improved mojo all over again—then ask yourself what you learned from this challenge.

Life hands you lessons constantly, and no one likes to have their plans and goals sidelined. As Witches and magicians, sometimes we assume that this sort of issue won't happen to us because, well…we work magick, damn it. Shouldn't we be immune or something?

But no matter who you are—be it Witch or mundane—when it comes to life, we all tend to enjoy the surprises we want. The surprises we *don't* enjoy are the ones we consider problems.

The best way to climb above this is to use your sense of humor. Make the best of the situation, and think outside of the box. Do some spell-craft troubleshooting. Correct mistakes you have made and work your new and improved spells with enthusiasm and verve!

As a magickal practitioner, you have resources and options other folks would not even dream of. If you find yourself in a tough financial spot, then take a moment and listen to your own intuition. Refer to the troubleshooting information in this chapter, and also go back and study those Hermetic laws at the beginning of the book. They are right at the beginning for an important reason: those principles are your foundation, and together we have built a strong and powerful magickal base.

Your magick will hold you. Don't give up!

Chapter Eight

Herbal & Crystal Magick for Abundance, Good Luck & Prosperity

All prosperity begins in the mind and is dependent
only on the full use of our creative imagination.

RUTH ROSS

Working with items from nature is a commonsense approach to magick. In both herbal and crystal magick, the plant or stone is a natural item that is valued for its magickal properties and the type of vibration it produces. Stones and herbs have many various types of energies, and for this chapter we will focus on those aligned with good luck, prosperity, success, and abundance. If you wish to reconnect to your earth religion, these two types of practical magick will show you the way.

Herb and crystal magick is very practical. It is also personal. Each individual will develop his or her own way of connecting to and working with herbs and crystals. This individual style and relationship that you develop will only help to strengthen your PME and therefore the successful results of your spellwork. By incorporating these suggested magickal herbs and stones—many of which I am betting you already have on hand—you can also save some money. Apply the information from this chapter and get creative! Use this magickal knowledge as a springboard for conjuring up even more kinds of practical spells for prosperity and abundance.

A Witch's Dozen of Herbs for Prosperity Magick

*...the soul of the real garden lies in the perfect
prosperity of the plants of which it is the home.*

GEORGE SITWELL

These featured thirteen herbs are classic components used in prosperity magick. Most of these are easy to locate at a garden center, in the garden, or growing in your yard. Save some money and use earthy supplies when possible. Look at what you have on hand in the kitchen or growing in the garden. I bet you have more herbal magick supplies than you realize!

For example, try sprinkling a little dried chamomile onto your applications and paperwork at work for success. Carry a piece of fragrant cedar wood to attract money, or dust a tiny pinch of ground cinnamon around your office, place of business, or home to attract good luck—simple, discreet, practical, and very, very effective.

You will find a few charm verses in this section, as well as an herbal circle casting for any prosperity ritual. You can easily add the circle casting to any of the spells in this book or ones of your own creation. For even more information on herb magick (and plenty of herbal spells), refer to my books *Garden Witchery*, *Garden Witch's Herbal*, *Book of Witchery*, and *Herb Magic for Beginners*.

> **Bay** (*Lauris nobilis*): Also called sweet bay, it is an ancient herb of victory and success. Bay leaf crowns were given to the victors at Greek and Roman sporting events. This solar herb is sacred to the god Apollo. Bay can also remove negativity from your spellwork, so this would be a clever addition to any herbal magick worked during a waning moon.
>
> Using a gold pen, write your wish for success on a bay leaf and then burn the leaf in a candle's flame to make your wish become a reality.

Repeat this charm while you (carefully) burn the leaf:

*Bay leaf, bay leaf, please now grant me my desire for success
As the leaf is consumed by the flame, my magick manifests.*

The planetary association for bay is the sun; its elemental correspondence is fire.

Cinquefoil (*Potentilla anserina*): Also called "five finger grass," this pretty perennial herb comes in many varieties for the home garden. Add cinquefoil to prosperity spells to encourage abundance and good health. This herb encourages you to grab that brass ring and follow your dreams! When it is added to sachet and herbal charm bags, it attracts wealth and prosperity. The planetary association is Jupiter, and the elemental correspondence is earth.

Clover (White) (*Trifolium repens*): This "herb" is often found growing wild in the suburban lawn. The typical three-leaf clover is sacred to the Triple Goddess and also to the Celtic goddess Brigid. A four-leaf clover encourages good fortune and money magick. According to the language of flowers, the white clover signifies good luck and hard work. Add a four-leaf clover to your shoe and good luck and prosperity are thought to walk with you. The clever clover also ensures the blessing of the faeries on your prosperity magick. The planetary association for the white clover is Mercury, and the elemental correspondence is air.

Dandelion: The homey dandelion flower and its foliage are worked into spells and herbal charms for success, creativity, and to grant wishes. The dandelion is associated with the summer solstice and faery magick. As every child knows, pluck a dandelion head when it has gone to seed, make your wish, and blow. To kick that magick up a few notches, call upon the sylphs, the elemental creatures of the air, and they will carry your wishes for prosperity off and out on the summer breeze. Doing this simple magick on the night of a full moon will increase its magickal effect. The planetary association for the dandelion is the sun, and the elemental correspondence is air.

High John the Conqueror Root (*Impomea jalapa*): This plant is related to the morning glory and the sweet potato. When in bloom, the plant resembles a red morning glory. It is the root, however, that is wildly popular in American folk magick. This root is carried for success, wealth, and victory. The root needs to be whole to be effective; chips and pieces of High John the Conqueror are best suited to be blended into oils or potions. The whole root works especially well in men's magick and is a potent herbal charm to carry with you on job interviews, no matter what your gender. A gambler's herb, it is typically added to charm bags and carried as a prosperity talisman. Try wrapping a dollar bill around the root and securing it with a green ribbon. The planetary associations are the sun and Mars, and the elemental correspondence is fire.

Hollyhock (*Althea rosa*): These old-fashioned cottage-style biennials attract prosperity and faery magick. Hollyhocks come in an array of colors with both single- and double-flowering varieties. Yellow, pink, red, white, and almost black colors are available. In the language of flowers, the hollyhock symbolizes richness, fertility, and ambition. If you plant hollyhocks in your garden, the faeries will bless all who dwell in the home with luck and success. Carry the seedpods in your pocket or add them to prosperity-themed charm bags. The planetary association for the hollyhock is Venus, and the elemental correspondence is water.

Honeysuckle (*Lonicera* spp.): This is classified as a semi-evergreen shrub. According to herbal folklore, to have a honeysuckle growing near your home is to invite good luck and prosperity into your life. One of the easiest to obtain and yet more powerful prosperity herbs, the tenacious honeysuckle should be used generously in your magick. Tuck a few honeysuckle blossoms into your pocket or wallet to attract money, for as surely as bees are attracted to the honeysuckle's heady scent, money and opportunities will be drawn to you. (You can wear honeysuckle-scented perfume for the same purpose.) The honeysuckle plant is so linked into prosperity and magick that I had it included in the illustration for the Ace of Pentacles in the *Witches Tarot*. The planetary association for the honeysuckle is Jupiter, and the elemental correspondence is earth.

Mint (*Mentha* spp.): A fragrant, fast-spreading perennial herb. Mint is sacred to both Hades/Pluto and Hecate. Growing mint in the garden is a sure-fire way to attract prosperity to your home. Keep in mind that mint is an aggressive herb and spreads quickly. It can take over a garden if you are not careful, so I suggest that you keep mint corralled by planting it in containers. Mint brings sparkle and harmony to prosperity spellwork. A fresh leaf or two can be tucked into your pocket or purse to attract cash. Mint can also bring a breath of fresh air to financial projects and goals. The planetary associations are Pluto, Venus, and Mercury, and the elemental correspondence is air.

Money Plant (*Lunaria*): Also called honesty and the silver dollar plant, this pretty plant attracts wealth. The seed pods resemble silvery coins and are incorporated into charm bags. Here is an herbal spell to work with Lunaria. Add a seed pod to the bottom of a clear candleholder, then burn an enchanted and empowered green votive candle on top of it to help draw money. For best results, work this herb magick during a full moon. Here is a spell to go with it:

> *Lunaria, silver dollar plant, draw money now to me*
> *Under a full moon so bright, please bless me with prosperity!*

Allow the votive candle to burn in a safe place until it goes out on its own. Tucking the little round seed pods into charm bags or your pocket or wallet will have the same money-drawing effect. The planetary association for Lunaria is obviously the moon, and the elemental correspondence is the earth.

Oak (*Quercus* spp.): The deciduous oak tree is associated with many sky gods such as Zeus, Jupiter, and Thor. It is hardly a surprise, then, to learn that the oak in all its many wondrous varieties is also aligned with thunder and lightning. A long-lived species of tree, the oak may reach up to 150 feet in height. Oaks were often used as sentinels or as markers to denote a magickal place. According to folklore, wearing a chaplet or crown of fresh oak leaves will grant you wisdom as well as special notice from the thunder gods. The fruit of the oak tree, the acorn, is a simple pocket talisman for growth and prosperity and is a promise of things to come. Adding acorns and small, fresh oak leaves to your prosperity spells and charm bags will not only boost your creativity, they will also help you to gain the favor of the sky gods who have claimed the oak as their sacred tree. The planetary association for the oak is Jupiter, and the elemental correspondence is fire.

Pine (*Pinus* spp.): The pine tree is a coniferous evergreen. There are many varieties of the long-lived pine tree, and it is sacred to many deities such as Pan, Venus, Dionysus, Bacchus, and Astarte. The evergreen pine is linked with midwinter festivities and the rebirth of the sun. In the language of flowers, the pine tree symbolizes longevity, endurance, and warmth—all excellent qualities to work into your prosperity spells. The fruit of the pine tree, the cone, is symbolic of abundance and fertility, while pine needles banish negativity and break hexes. The classic planetary association for all pines is Mars, and the elemental correspondence is air.

Shamrock (*Oxalis*): This popular houseplant, also known as the blooming shamrock plant, should not be confused with the white clover. You will find plenty of these perky houseplants sold as seasonal potted plants around St. Patrick's Day. In the language of flowers, the shamrock symbolizes good luck and lightheartedness. Pick up a blooming shamrock this spring to add a bit of the "luck of the Irish" to your herbal prosperity spells and charms. The shamrock is associated with the Triple Goddess and Celtic magick. Magickally, the shamrock brings health, good luck, and money, and it encourages fame and success. The planetary association is Venus, and the elemental correspondence is earth.

Sunflower (*Helianthus annus*): The stately sunflower is sacred to many solar deities such as Helios, Apollo, Brigid, and Sunna. This flower is grown as an annual and has become wildly popular in the florist's trade in recent years. These days sunflowers come in all sizes and colors, but the magickal meaning remains the same. The sunflower symbolizes success and fame. If you need to stand out in a crowd—whether that's for a job application or applying to school or scholarships and so forth—working with the sunflower in your herbal magick is a smart choice. You may add the petals of sunflowers to charm bags or tuck several stems into a sturdy vase and add them to your prosperity altar setup.

You may also work with the seeds of the sunflower. Casting a prosperity magick circle with sunflower seeds (outdoors, of course) would be a lovely way of giving back to the powers of nature. Here is a circle-casting verse for you to try. Time this magick for sunrise to tap into the power of a new day and fresh beginnings. As you cast your ritual circle, scatter the sunflower seeds in the grass. Begin in the east and work your way around the circle in a clockwise direction. Say:

Beginning in the east, this circle of sunflower seeds is cast
May my prosperity spell flourish today and my magick last.
My wishes will bloom and my prosperity grow with all certainty
I now generously give so that I can abundantly receive.

Now work your chosen prosperity spell. When the spell is done, leave the sunflower seeds as they are and allow the birds to gobble them up—that way, as you generously give so shall you abundantly receive. The sunflower's planetary association is the sun, and its elemental correspondence is fire.

Herbal Charm Bag Magick for Prosperity

For a naturally powerful type of prosperity magick that can be worked successfully regardless of the phase of the moon, create an herbal charm bag. Remember: if the moon is waxing, then pull the prosperity and success toward you. If the moon is waning, then use the charm bag to push away lack, need, and financial difficulties.

Peruse the previous list and choose the botanicals that resonate with you or that you can most easily acquire. For this spell, you will need to gather your chosen fresh herbs, a six-inch square of fabric, and a coordinating colored ribbon to tie the bundle together. (I suggest green for prosperity and good luck or gold for wealth and success.) Or you may prefer to use the pre-made sheer organza bridal favor bags. These sheer, small organza bags are found in the bridal section of arts and crafts stores and make clever and quick charm bag alternatives for folks who do not sew. For prosperity magick, look for bags in dark green, pale green, metallic gold, or all-purpose white.

Place your herbal ingredients into the premade bags and draw the ribbons tightly together, then tie three knots. If you are using a square of fabric, gather up each corner and make a small bundle. Wrap the ribbon around the bundle and then secure it with three knots. Then say:

> With all the power of three times three
> Goddess, bless my herbal sorcery!

If the moon is waxing (from new to full), say these lines next:

> By *waxing moon, my prosperity shall increase*
> A *positive change will my magick now release!*

Or, if the moon is waning (day after full moon to new moon), say these lines next:

> By *waning moon, financial problems shall decrease*
> A *positive change will my magick now release!*

Now hold the herbal charm bag in the palm of your hand and enchant it by infusing it with your own personal power. Hold firmly in your mind the image of happiness, prosperity, good luck, and success. Build up those positive thoughtforms and put the law of attraction to work! When you feel the charm bag start to warm up in your hands, repeat the following spell verse:

> *Magickal herbs of prosperity and power*
> I *conjure you to assist me in this hour.*
> Add *your natural magick gently to mine*
> Bringing *wealth and success to me at all times.*
> By *the enchantment of herbs, this spell has been spun*
> As I *will, so mote it be, and let it harm none.*

Pocket the herbal charm bag and keep it with you on your person for one month. After the time has passed, open up the bag and return the herbal components neatly to nature. Wash the fabric and ribbons (or organza favor bag) by hand and allow them to air-dry so you can reuse them at another time.

A Witch's Dozen of Crystals for Abundance, Success, and Prosperity

These gems have life in them: their colors
speak, say what words fail of.

GEORGE ELIOT

What is it about crystals, stones, and gems? They speak to us on an elemental level. Almost all Witches have a collection of tumbled stones; I have yet to meet one who doesn't have a dish of tumbled stones or a few crystals sitting out somewhere. Crystal magick is one of the first magicks we typically work with and appreciate.

There is a wealth of power in the earth and the stones, gems, and crystals that come from it. Here is a quick list of some of my favorite prosperity-enhancing stones. These featured stones are typically easy to find—just check your local metaphysical store and peruse their selection of tumbled stones. These stones are listed in alphabetical order with a brief description of their magickal associations. Consider how you could employ these down-to-earth prosperity tools in your witchery. You could wear the stones as jewelry, tuck a few tumbled stones in your pocket or purse, add stones to a charm bag or herbal sachet for more power, or surround a spell candle with stones. There are dozens of creative and practical ways to use crystals and stones in your spellwork.

Aventurine: This soft, sparkly green stone is an all-around good luck stone. It is money attracting and often called the gambler's stone. Aventurine will help you recognize details that others may miss; it can also enhance your latent leadership qualities, and it encourages creativity and perseverance. This stone boosts your health and may also ward off any pesky emotional vampires at your job. Its planetary association is Mercury, and its elemental correspondence is air.

Bloodstone: Bloodstone is green chalcedony marbled with red spots. This stone is for good health, wealth, and to promote a sense of victory. Place a tumbled stone in a cash register to attract a full cash drawer. Another interesting magickal property of the bloodstone is that it relieves depression and promotes healing, which makes it an excellent choice to work with if you are feeling down about your financial situation. Use the bloodstone to help build more positive thoughtforms and as you begin to put the law of attraction to work in your life.

Empower your bloodstones with this charm. Raise your PME and hold the bloodstones in the palm of your hand. Visualize what it is that you need them to do. Program the stones with your focus and your magickal goal. Say:

> *The bloodstone removes negativity*
> *May its magick cleanse and purify me.*
> *As the bloodstone's power removes anger and strife*
> *This spell brings victory and wealth into my life.*

The planetary association of the bloodstone is Mars, and the elemental correspondence is fire.

Chrysoprase: This apple-green form of chalcedony encourages creativity and will bring your talents to the surface. If you carry a small piece with you, it will draw in prosperity. Chrysoprase promotes cheer as well as reduces envy, greed, and tension in a work environment. This pretty crystal also helps keep customers and employees loyal. The planetary association is Venus, and the elemental correspondence is earth.

Citrine: This solar crystal is a potent cleanser and energizer. A wonderful stone to promote abundance, it assists you in both attracting and manifesting wealth into your life. Citrine promotes self-confidence, prosperity, and success. This is a stone of sunshine and joy; it is good for ridding yourself of the blues. This fabulous stone promotes inner tranquility, which then allows wisdom to guide your way. Put a cluster of citrine on your desk at home or at work and allow it to cleanse the atmosphere, ridding it of any negative thoughtforms. The planetary association is the sun, and the elemental correspondence is fire.

Emerald: This precious stone is one of the most expensive on the market today, so I suggest working with emerald jewelry that you already own or using low-grade uncut stones for your crystal magick. This stone encourages successful partnerships and lasting friendships. It can help bring groups of people together and ensure that they work together as a team, making emeralds perfect for business spells. This gem improves clairvoyant abilities and can help you open up to receiving wisdom from the universe. Finally, the emerald is said to strengthen the character and to attract positive realities. The planetary association is Venus, and the elemental correspondence is earth.

Jade (Green): Jade is said to help you discover your own inner beauty and self-worth. If you empower a jade piece of jewelry and wear it every day, it will attract prosperous energies into your life. Jade helps clear the air and encourages a healthier attitude about money. This quietly emotional stone will draw harmony, wisdom, and friendship into your life. Finally, green jade is thought to help you channel your passions in new and positive ways. The planetary association is Venus, and the elemental correspondence is water.

Green Tourmaline: Also known as verdelite, this stone is for fresh starts and creativity. It will boost your herb and garden magick. Tourmaline is a healing stone that promotes self-confidence and good health. It is considered to be a receptive stone, so wearing it as jewelry can help you draw in prosperity and happiness. Finally, green tourmaline helps transform negative energy and thought-forms into positive ones.

Here is a simple spell verse for you to enchant your green tourmaline jewelry or tumbled stone. This will create a talisman—an object created for a specific magickal purpose and one that will transform negative energy into positive.

> I call on the tourmaline in shades of deepest green
> Now transform negative to positive energy.
> This gemstone boosts my self-confidence and makes me smile
> I'll be prosperous and healthy for a good long while.

Lepidolite: Carrying this sparkling lavender-pink and purple colored stone will bring good luck to the bearer; it is a calming, spiritual stone. Lepidolite is thought to reduce stress and doubt, and it has peaceful qualities. Another stone that encourages optimism, it also attracts good fortune. Furthermore, lepidolite can help remove emotional blocks to your magickal goals. It can help you learn to stand on your own and attain financial independence. The planetary associations are Jupiter and Neptune, and the elemental correspondence is water.

Malachite: The banded malachite is a gorgeous stone, popular in jewelry and easily obtainable in pretty tumbled stone pieces. Worn to improve your energy during magick work, it can also increase your PME and give your prosperity spells a big boost. Called the salesman's stone, it is often placed in cash register drawers to pull in sales. Malachite is also worked into crystal spells to heal depression and for general health purposes. If your malachite stone should suddenly break, it is a warning of danger. The planetary association is Venus, and the elemental correspondence is earth.

Moss Agate: The moss agate is intimately linked to the earth and is thought to grant you the power to see the inherent beauty in all of nature. A translucent stone with green, cloudy, mosslike markings, this is the ideal talisman for gardeners, landscapers, conservationists, wildlife biologists, even florists—anyone who makes their living working with plants and nature. The moss agate is a stone of success and one linked with prosperity and abundance magick. It can bolster your self-esteem and would be a handy stone to have in your pocket during an interview or at a big meeting at work, as the moss agate enhances communication and reduces stress. It can also reinforce the bearer's ability to get along well with others. The planetary association is Mercury, and the elemental correspondence is earth.

Rhodochrosite: A beautiful banded stone in shades of pink with white, gray, and black. This is a stone of love and compassion. You may be wondering why it is included here in a prosperity stone listing. Rhodochrosite helps us learn from past mistakes and keeps our heart open. Recall the LOA: if you want to attract positive things into your life, then you need to be in an emotionally positive and upbeat frame of mind. This stone soothes stress and helps to lessen anxiety. This gorgeous pink stone also enhances creativity. It brings happiness and joy into your world. Its planetary association is Mars (some say Venus), and its elemental correspondence is fire.

Tiger's-eye: The golden-brown banded tiger's-eye stone is classically used to promote prosperity and cash. It is an energy boosting, courageous stone, and it has protective attributes as well. Tiger's-eye will ward off jealous feelings from your detractors, as well as help you to stay grounded and complete your goals. Readily available as jewelry or as an affordable tumbled stone, tiger's-eye is excellent for removing blocks of any kind, and it can assist a person who is trying to make more positive choices in their life. The planetary association is the sun, and the elemental correspondence is fire.

Turquoise: A classic good luck charm. Turquoise can help success and prosperity to manifest in your life. This pretty blue-green stone attracts new friends and is believed to unite the energies of Mother Earth and Father Sky. If turquoise jewelry is given as a gift, it blesses the recipient with affluence and joy. Try working prosperity spells with turquoise at the time of the new crescent moon.

Here is a quick crystal spell that combines the energies of the newly waxing moon phase and the turquoise stone.

Time the spell for shortly after sunset, when the thin crescent waxing moon is in the western sky. To begin, hold a piece of turquoise firmly in the palm of your hand. Raise your personal magickal energy and wait until you feel the stone start to warm up. Then move outdoors and look up at the moon. Hold the stone up to the moon so it seems surrounded by either side of the waxing crescent, then say:

> By the goddess Diana's crescent moon
> I ask the Maiden to grant me a boon.
> Empower this gem with prosperity
> May this turquoise stone's magick stay with me.

Keep the stone with you for one month. You may recharge it again at the next waxing crescent moon if you wish. The planetary association of turquoise is both Venus and Neptune, while the elemental correspondence is earth.

A Crystal Spell for Success and Good Luck

Read the following directions carefully and decide for yourself how you can personalize this crystal spell to make it more powerfully unique.

Timing: It is strongly recommended that this spell be worked during a waxing moon phase. Also keep in mind that there are two days of the week that are most opportune for prosperity magick: Sunday, which corresponds to the sun, success, wealth, and fame, and Thursday, which aligns to the planet Jupiter, prosperity, and abundance. Again, I do suggest working this spell during the waxing moon phase to take advantage of that growing and increasing energy. Or you may choose to tap into a full moon for the ultimate magickal power. In a perfect world you would have a full moon on a Sunday or a Thursday, but you certainly will have a couple of Sundays or Thursdays each month during that waxing moon period. Consult your astrological calendar and start plotting! Ultimately it will be up to you, but I find that a little preparation and taking the time to work during the most opportune moment to be well worth the wait.

Supplies:

- 4 crystals associated with prosperity
- a green candle (votive, taper, or mini) and a coordinating candleholder
- a lighter or matches
- your altar or a safe, flat surface

Directions: Pick up the unlit green candle. You may carve it at this time with whatever magickal symbol you prefer. Try the symbol of the sun ($\odot$) if you are casting on a Sunday or the symbol for Jupiter ($\Jupiter$) if casting this on a Thursday. If you are casting on the full moon, then carve whatever symbol you feel would be the most appropriate. As you engrave the candle, empower it with the following lines:

> As I hold this prosperity candle in my hands
> I empower it to send magick across the land.
> Now burn with purpose both bright and true
> May I be blessed in all that I do.

Place the enchanted candle in its holder and then light the candle. Arrange the four stones evenly in a circle around the candleholder. Repeat out loud what each stone is and what powers it brings to the spell. For example: "Malachite to boost my energy, tiger's-eye for power and courage, aventurine for good luck, and bloodstone for a full cash register drawer." You get the idea.

Now, once the crystals and stones are named and you have declared the energies they are bringing to the magick, then you can repeat the spell verse reverently, with intention and purpose. Say:

> Crystals of magick, good luck, and success
> By your powers I will surely be blessed.
> Your energies enhance my spell candle so green
> Good luck and prosperity send swiftly to me.
> The earthy power of the stones will anchor this spell
> While the candle's bright fire illuminates so well.
> By the light of the moon and the strength of the sun
> As I will, so mote it be, and let it harm none.

Allow the spell candle to burn in a safe place until it goes out on its own. Keep the four crystals with you for one month, then you may return them with your other supplies.

Blessed be.

Lastly, Consider This…

A Witch's greatest wealth is her ingenuity.

KALA TROBE

Now that you have this herbal and crystal information at your witchy fingertips, take a moment or two and go back through all the spells in the book from before this chapter. Yes, each and every one of them. I know, I know…I am a hard-ass. But do it anyway.

Okay, now that you have taken a look at all of those spells from the previous chapters, how do you think you could have added herbs, crystals, or both to all of those spells to enhance and personalize them? Making a spell uniquely your own and adding some personality into it is what separates an advanced or adept Witch from someone who just goes through the motions.

So here is my sincere and straight-up suggestion: put some effort into your Craft. Add some personality, originality, and effort into your prosperity work. You will get out of this type of magick whatever you are willing to put into it.

Chapter Nine

PRACTICAL MAGICK

The spiritual is the parent of the practical.

THOMAS CARLYLE

WHAT EXACTLY IS practical magick? Practical magick is also known as thaumaturgy, though you may never have heard it called that before. A couple of years ago I did a lecture on advancing your Craft, and when I launched into the topics of theurgy and thaumaturgy, folks looked at me like I had grown two heads. Hey, it's not all garden witchery *all* the time. While I do specialize in herb and green magick, I have other tricks up my witchy sleeves as well.

Perhaps you have come across these terms in your studies but have no idea how they apply to you and your own magickal practice. However, theurgy and thaumaturgy are terms that you should be familiar with—say hello to some of the core teachings of the Craft.

Back in the day, what separated Witches from ceremonial magicians or wizards was the type of magick they practiced. Ceremonial magicians practiced theurgy, also known as high magick, while Witches worked more practical and down-to-earth magick, and that was considered to be thaumaturgy. Consider the following descriptions.

Thaumaturgy is the use of magickal powers to influence or predict events. It can be defined as Witchcraft or conjuration. This type of magick is earthy and simple, and it relies on the use of natural items. Things like herb magick, crystal magick, candle magick, and sympathetic magick may be called low magick—or, more correctly, practical magick. The utilization of the energies and magick found in nature, and working with the seasons and cycles of the moon, is thaumaturgy. With thaumaturgy it is all about the results of your spellcrafting that come to be in the physical world.

Theurgy, on the other hand, is defined as rituals that are designed to align oneself with the Divine, or the angelic realms. Also known as high magick, theurgy is a type of magickal practice that has its emphasis placed on more spiritual goals and communing directly with the Divine. High magick often incorporates mathematics, astrology, alchemy, and the Kabbalah. Theurgy is about persuading, asking, or even bribing an angel or deity to do something for you. As you can imagine, extremely careful ritual practice is required for this. Theurgy is magick performed with the angels or the gods, where the angels or gods themselves intercede in human affairs.

Today, if you say the words "high magick" to many Witches, you might notice folks starting to get twitchy. The term high magick often makes people start to think of an eccentric, "boys only" sort of snooty magickal club. And honestly, there are folks out there who embrace that stereotype, but don't let that throw you off course. People who work high magick are simply ceremonial magicians, and you may have more in common with them than you might think. How is that, you may wonder? Well, you may be surprised to know that if you work with angelic magick or planetary energies and magick, then you are dipping your magickal toes into high magick as well.

Quick, go and check. No, the sky did not fall in. Oh, and will you look at that? The sun still rose in the east. I have yet to meet a magickal practitioner whose work did not overlap from theurgy to thaumaturgy and back again. They probably just never realized it. In today's magickal world there is no obvious separation of the practices of theurgy and thaumaturgy. Witches and magicians both practice these two types of magick. Once upon a time they may have been considered separate, but in modern times these magickal practices have come to flourish and grow together.

Author Christopher Penczak says this about the practice of theurgy and thaumaturgy: "Magick is magick regardless of the label you put on it. The power is in your hands and is your responsibility. But there is always a divine connection, whether you realize it or not."

Now, just to make things interesting and in an effort to expand your magickal prowess a bit, we are about to focus on planetary magick. It's true that planetary magick is classically not considered to be thaumaturgy. However, there are many practical applications to be explored here. Let me show you how to successfully combine these planetary energies into your prosperity spellwork.

Planetary Magick

He is the true enchanter whose spell operates not upon
the senses but upon the imagination and the heart.

WASHINGTON IRVING

To some modern magickal practitioners, planetary magick is considered to be a combination of energy, psychology, and spirit formulations. It is also thought that the planetary energies themselves could be considered concentrated Pagan deity energy. (After all, the planets were named after the old Roman gods.) Back in the day, the planets themselves were considered to be the physical body of the gods. That makes the planetary effects both psychological and archetypal when it comes to magick. To be clear, archetypes are universally understood symbols that have a mythical quality, such as Father, Mother, Sage, Crone, Hero, Warrior, Lover, and so on.

Now do you see why this information becomes important? Embrace the idea that your practical prosperity magick has layers and depth. It is not just burning green candles and repeating a bunch of clever spells composed in rhyming couplets; it is so much more. There is real and advanced information for you to build off of here. Think of how much you have learned so far about the Hermetic principles, the law of attraction, the four elements, thoughtforms, attracting abundance, herb and crystal magick, and your personal magickal energy.

Remember back in the introduction when I said that prosperity magick is a deceptively simple subject? Just stop and consider all of the knowledge that you have added to your magickal repertoire. To perform prosperity spells effectively, you truly need to have your heart open and be ready to receive knowledge. You also need to have your head in the game and be able to understand all of the subtleties this type of magick possesses.

In doing so, you will be moving up in the magickal world and becoming an adept. This energetic shift takes willingness and commitment. It's like I always say: the strongest, truest magick comes from both the mind and the heart.

Combine the following information on planetary magick with the practicality of thaumaturgy, then apply this with imagination and heart to your own spellcraft.

Jupiter

It is the stars, the stars above us,
which govern our conditions.

WILLIAM SHAKESPEARE

The planet Jupiter is the fifth from the sun and the largest planet in our solar system. Jupiter was known to astronomers in antiquity; the Romans named this large planet after their principal god, Jupiter. Jupiter was the king of the gods—a deity of thunder, lightning, and passion—so the name only makes sense considering the planet's size and the spectacular bright clouds and constant storms on its surface. Jupiter does have rings like Saturn and Uranus, and the great red spot on Jupiter's surface is a storm that has been brewing for over 300 years.

At last count there were at least sixty-seven moons orbiting Jupiter, including the four planet-sized Galilean moons named Io, Europa, Ganymede, and Callisto. Ganymede, the biggest of those four moons, is larger than both the planets Mercury and Pluto. Ganymede has the distinction of being the ninth largest object in the solar system. This massive moon was named after a lover of the Greek version of Jupiter, the god Zeus.

According to Greek mythology, Ganymede—a beautiful young man—was chosen by Zeus, brought to Olympus, and made immortal with the honor of being both a cup bearer to the gods and Zeus's lover. It's interesting to note that all four of the Galilean moons were labeled with the names of lovers or conquests of the Roman Jupiter or the Greek Zeus.

Astrologically the planet Jupiter represents wisdom. It influences expansion, growth, improvement, higher learning, and good fortune. One theory is that since Jupiter is the largest planet in our solar system, with its own cosmos of moons and rings orbiting it, it will influence and expand the effect of everything it comes into contact with.

Jupiter is the premier planetary energy for prosperity magick, with the capacity to attract what we most desire. When you work in harmony with Jupiter's energy, it is said that the blessings of prosperity, insight, increased personal power, and good health are yours.

The planet Jupiter is linked to sky gods such as the Roman Jupiter, Greek Zeus, and Norse Thor. Jupiter's planetary energy has a natural affinity with leadership, teaching, prosperity, advancement, and benevolent powers. The practical magickal correspondences for Jupiter are as follows:

Correspondences for Jupiter

Magickal Uses: prosperity, abundance, practical magick, leadership, good health, healing, wish magick

Sigil: ♃

Day of the Week: Thursday

Tarot Cards: the Emperor, the Wheel of The Year/Wheel of Fortune, Ace of Pentacles

Natural Symbols: lightning, oak leaf, acorn, crown of oak leaves, the cornucopia from Althea the nanny goat, the cup of abundance from Ganymede

Animals: eagle, swan, hippogriff

Element: water

Deities: Jupiter, Juno Moneta, Zeus, Thor

Archangel: Sachiel, whose day is Thursday and whose flower is the violet; you may call on him in matters of justice, the law, wealth, victory, keeping a sense of humor, and for kindness

Angel of Jupiter: Zadkiel for benevolence and good fortune; burn frankincense to attract his attention

Metal: tin, zinc

Colors: royal blue, green, purple

Trees: oak, juniper, linden, maple

Herbs: anise, borage, cinquefoil, clove, dandelion, fig, honeysuckle, hyssop, meadowsweet, nutmeg, sage

Crystals and Gems: sapphire, lapis lazuli, amethyst, turquoise, labradorite, aquamarine

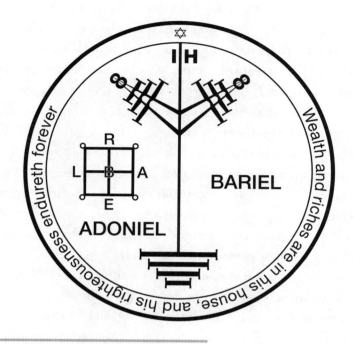

The Fourth Pentacle of Jupiter

The key to success is to never stop learning.
The key to failure is to think you know it all.

AUTHOR UNKNOWN

I am including some information here about one of my favorite planetary pentacles from *The Key of Solomon*, specifically the Fourth Pentacle of Jupiter. These seals or pentacles of the planets are talismans, and they are based on the seven ancient "planets." These pentacles are regularly employed by Witches today, and the planetary pentacles do work out very nicely for thaumaturgy (practical magick).

I have been using the Fourth Pentacle of Jupiter for decades in my practical spells and prosperity work, and I have to admit that the results are pretty exciting. When you work with any of the pentacles from *The Key of Solomon*, you are discovering the magick of symbolism.

Think of the Fourth Pentacle of Jupiter as a key—a key to your higher self, if you will. This allows you to have a deeper connection to your planetary magick. It's not unlike taking a key to unlock a door—in this case, it would be a door in your mind. When you see the Fourth Pentacle of Jupiter, your mind clicks over to a different level of awareness. Also, the repeated use of a symbol (such as our featured Fourth Pentacle of Jupiter) will build up power over time.

Think of it like the batteries in your cell phone: the power is on hand and ready to use whenever you need it, so you can use this specific planetary pentacle as a key to trigger your mind for a specific purpose; in this case, to draw prosperity into your life. When these pentacles are created, enchanted, carried, or used, they are thought to change your circumstances. These pentacles can attract blessings and banish negativity. They can also boost your magickal power, again depending on the individual planetary pentacle you are working with.

As I wrote about in *Practical Protection Magick* (Llewellyn, 2011), you can work with the pentacles from *The Key of Solomon* and still keep your magick practical and straightforward. To start, print the Fourth Pentacle of Jupiter on your home printer on complementary colored paper. For this I would suggest pale blue paper or, if you want to go old school, then try reproducing the image in blue ink on parchment. (Blue is a Jupiter color and is definitely the way to go when creating this prosperity-inducing magickal pentacle.)

When I print out a pentacle at home, I neatly cut out the symbol and glue it on a seven-day jar candle to boost my magick. I have also been known to run those pentacles (printed on colored paper) through my repositionable sticker-maker machine and then apply the pentacles exactly where I want them. This way I can adhere the prosperity-inducing pentacle to my wallet, my desk, or my checkbook cover. If you prefer to keep things more classic and permanent, then you can carefully transfer the design by hand and in blue ink to a three-inch wooden disc purchased from the local arts and crafts store.

Please be aware that magickal timing is an essential part to creating this pentacle, so I do strongly recommend working on the day of the week associated with the astrological body in the title of the pentacle. In this case, the Fourth Pentacle of Jupiter *must* be created on a Thursday, Jupiter's day.

If you do a search for this pentacle online, you will likely find a gorgeous symbol surrounded by Hebrew lettering. I do not read Hebrew, and I will admit that it makes me twitchy not to know exactly what any magickal symbol or lettering translates to. So I did a little digging and found that the words around the pentacle translate to "wealth and riches are in his house, and his righteousness endureth forever."

The pentacle on page 173 is the English-language version that I re-created onto a wooden disc for myself. I have been using it successfully for over twenty years.

To re-create this Fourth Pentacle of Jupiter for yourself, I suggest that you sketch the image lightly in pencil first and make sure that it is perfect. Be sure to draw it on the proper day, Thursday. Take your time, and once you have the sketch finished to your liking, then carefully go over it in permanent blue ink.

For my own permanent pentacle, I added the English translation around the outside, as I could not manage the Hebrew lettering. Also, the word on the right side of the pentacle is the angelic name Bariel. The word under the square on the left is another angelic name: Adoniel. On the backside of my own wooden pentacle I have a large Jupiter symbol drawn in blue ink, smack-dab in the center. An inscribed wooden pentacle makes for a nice visual symbol to incorporate into your spellcraft, or even as a portable type of charm to carry with you.

Here is a spell verse that you can use to bind the magick of your newly created Fourth Pentacle of Jupiter firmly to you. Yes, this also must be worked on a Thursday. I suggest doing this right after you finish creating your permanent Fourth Pentacle of Jupiter.

Hold the newly created pentacle in your hands and say out loud exactly what you need it to do—in this case, to draw wealth, wisdom, and prosperity correctly to you. Then repeat the following spell verse:

> *Practical witchery combined with the magick of old*
> *To use this enchantment successfully, one must be bold.*
> *Made on Jupiter's day, now the magick begins*
> *Combining wealth, success, and magickal wisdom.*
> *I now blend my magick with this pentacle of power*
> *May it bring to me prosperity in every hour.*

I hope you enjoy working with this pentacle from *The Key of Solomon*. It can really add power and punch to your practical prosperity magick.

The Sun

No matter how dark the night, somehow the sun
rises once again and all shadows are chased away.

DAVID MATTHEW

Blazing at the center of our solar system, the sun illuminates all. Deified and venerated throughout time, the sun has been seen as a god or the principal god in various religions. Kings once ruled by the power of the sun and claimed descent from it. A symbol of divine power, the sun is the bringer of life and light. Our closest star, the sun is thought to have been formed over four and a half billion years ago. Without it, there would be no life here on earth. The corona around the sun is its extended outer atmosphere. Science tells us that the corona is actually larger than the sun itself. The corona constantly expands into space and forms a solar wind that fills the entire solar system. It is also interesting to note that the sun's color is actually white but appears yellow to us here on earth because of our blue atmosphere.

The sun is the most important planet in personal astrology. It represents our conscious mind and tells us who we are and where we are going. Your birth sign is, in fact, your sun sign. It is from the sun that we derive our identity, and it is thought that the sun shows us what we are learning to be. Take a look at the personality traits of your own sun sign to see what lessons the sun has for you.

Furthermore, the sun's golden light blesses us with strength, vitality, energy, and the will to succeed. It represents that spark of creativity, and it grants us the power to rise and meet any challenge. From a magickal perspective, the sun symbolizes the divine spark that is carried inside all of us.

In Greek and Roman mythology, the sun was represented by the god Helios, one of the Titans. Eventually Helios came to represent the physical sun traveling across the sky, while the Greco-Roman god Apollo became associated with healing, prophecy, knowledge, and light.

> **Practical Magick Note:** Keep in mind that in ancient times the classic magickal astrological system was determined by Ptolemy. He used the five planets that were visible to the naked eye and the sun and the moon. Hence the sun, our closest star, became rolled up in planetary magick.

Correspondences for the Sun

Magickal Uses: success, wealth, increase, fame, riches, practical magick, achieving personal goals, unconquerable power, regeneration

Sigil: ☉

Day of the Week: Sunday

Tarot Cards: the Sun, the Chariot, Strength

Natural Symbols: the sun, a sunflower

Animals: lion, phoenix, hawk, winged horse

Element: fire

Deities: Helios, Apollo, Brigid, Divine Sun Child, Ra, Sunna

Archangel: Michael, whose day is Sunday and flower is the marigold; you can call on him for strength, divine protection, truth, and illumination

Metal: gold

Colors: yellow, gold

Associated Trees: ash, bay laurel, oak, rowan, witch hazel

Herbs: agave, angelica, calendula, carnation, chamomile, cinnamon, frankincense, marigold, mistletoe, orange, peony, rosemary, rue, St. John's wort, sunflower

Crystals and Gems: citrine, diamond, sunstone, tiger's-eye, topaz, yellow jasper, zircon

A Solitary Sunrise Ritual for Success and Prosperity

Timing: Work this solitary ritual on a Sunday at sunrise.

Supplies:

- a yellow or gold votive candle
- a straight pin or boline (for inscribing the candle)
- a votive candleholder
- a plain, small plate or saucer
- magnetic golden sand
- matches or a lighter
- the Sun and Strength cards from your tarot deck
- fresh solar flowers such as sunflowers, yellow carnations, marigolds, and fresh oak leaves
- a vase filled with fresh water

- crystals such as tiger's-eye, citrine, and yellow jasper
- a small towel
- a safe, flat surface

Directions: This spell has specific timing and instructions to help raise your personal magickal energy. Set up your work area so you face the east and the rising sun about a half-hour before sunrise. Outdoors is best, but in a pinch use an eastern-facing window indoors.

As the sun breaks the horizon, raise your arms to it and drink in the light. There is magick to be tapped into at the birth of a new day. Soak up some solar energy for a few minutes and get ready to direct this energy into your spellwork.

When you feel you are ready, place the votive candleholder in the center of the small plate. Pour a thin circle of golden magnetic sand on the saucer, around the outside of the candleholder. Wipe your hands clean of the sand. Arrange the rest of the spell's components on your altar in a way you find pleasing. Keep the tarot cards and the flowers well away from the candle.

Next, inscribe and empower your candle with the pin or your boline with the astrological symbol of the sun: ☉. Center yourself and shift your mood to a positive and upbeat one. Empower the spell candle by holding the inscribed candle in your hands and up so the rising sun shines upon it, then repeating the candle empowerment verse:

> As I *hold this prosperity candle in my hands*
> I *empower it to send magick across the land.*
> Now *burn with purpose, your flame strong, bright, and true*
> I *will be successful in all that* I *do.*

Set the inscribed and empowered candle in its holder and then light the candle. Repeat the following ritual verse with intention and purpose.

At first light on the sun's own day, this sunrise spell begins
As the light grows, my candles burn and magick starts to spin.
Flowers and stones of the sun, lend your powers now to me
Blending together toward my goals in strength and harmony.
Golden magnetic sand attracts success to all I say and do
Tarot cards will aid my focus and make my magick strong and true.
Now combine and ripple out, create change for all the world to see
This golden light blesses me now with success, wealth, and energy.

Allow the candle to burn in a safe place until it goes out on its own. Once the candle is spent, you may return the tarot cards to the deck. Pocket the stones for a few days to keep that solar energy going. The flowers you may keep in a place of prominence until they begin to fade, then return them neatly to nature by putting them in with your yard waste to be recycled or adding them to your compost pile.

A Witch's Dozen of Deities for Prosperity Magick

Deities bless the diligent.

SAM VEDA

Here is some information on thirteen deities associated with abundance, wealth, and prosperity. This information will come in handy as you create prosperity spells and charms of your own design. You will find a bit of information on the pantheon and the deity's specialties. Also, there are associated colors and, if applicable, stone, crystal, metal, and herbal correspondences to be used in their magick.

Abuntania (Roman): The goddess of the earth's abundance. She was also identified as Rosmerta and is often portrayed holding a basket of fruit. *Colors:* green and gold. *Metal:* gold. *Crystal:* moss agate. *Herbs:* wheat, corn, all fruits and grains.

Bona Dea (Roman): The "Good Goddess" of prosperity, abundance, and women's fertility, she is a mother goddess, often depicted with a cornucopia, a bowl, and a snake coiled around her right arm. The snake is a symbol of healing and regeneration. One of her festivals was held on May first. *Colors:* gold and purple. *Metal:* gold. *Crystal:* amethyst. *Herbs:* grapevines and grapes.

Cerridwen (Welsh): The goddess of manifestation, inspiration, shapeshifting, and wisdom. Cerridwen is a crone goddess. Her symbols include her cauldron of transformation and the waning moon. She would be wonderful to call on to banish poverty and bad luck. *Colors:* black and green. *Metal:* iron. *Crystal:* jet. *Herb:* corn.

Dagda (Proto-Celtic): Dagda, the generous and kind father god of Ireland, is the protector of his people. Dagda owns an overflowing cauldron that never empties. He is associated with generosity, wealth, and regeneration. *Colors:* green and brown. *Metal:* bronze.

Demeter/Ceres (Greco-Roman): A mother goddess of grain, agriculture, and the harvest, she is a benevolent deity with a temper. Demeter/Ceres is responsible for the changing seasons. As she mourns for her daughter Persephone while she is in the underworld for part of each year, the earth turns cold and winter begins. When Persephone returns to her mother, spring begins. If you are growing a garden, Demeter/Ceres is the one to call on. *Colors:* gold, green, and red. *Crystals:* agate, green tourmaline, and malachite. *Herbs:* wheat and the poppy.

Fortuna (Roman): The goddess of happiness and good fortune, Fortuna is known as the one who turns the wheel of the year. She is a goddess of fate and chance, and is often portrayed as a winged woman balancing on a globe or with the wheel of fortune and an overflowing cornucopia. To the Greeks, this goddess is known as Tyche. See chapter 5 for a spell with Fortuna. *Colors:* green, gold, and silver. *Metals:* gold, silver, and bronze. *Crystals:* amazonite and aventurine.

Freyr (Norse): Freyr is an agricultural god. Associated with peace, pleasure, virility, and prosperity, he is the brother of the goddess Freya. Freyr makes sure all of your material needs are met. *Color:* green. *Crystals:* jade and malachite. *Herbs:* wheat, corn, barley, and any grain.

Gaia (Greek): The primal earth mother. As the personification of the earth, all prosperity work is under her domain. Gaia is the mother of the Titans. She adds a bountiful, earthy, and rich energy to your magick. *Colors:* green and brown. *Crystals:* green agate, malachite, and jade. *Herbs:* all plant life.

Ganesha (Hindu): This elephant-headed, much-loved deity is a remover of obstacles and is associated with wealth and good luck. He is popular with merchants, traders, and students. Be sure to call on him for help with applications, scholarships, and grants. See chapters 4 and 7 for more information and spells featuring Ganesha. *Colors:* yellow and red. *Metal:* gold. *Crystal:* yellow sapphire. *Herb:* marigold.

Juno Moneta (Roman): One of the aspects of Juno. Juno Moneta presided over the Roman mint; see chapter 6 for more information. *Colors:* peacock blue, gold, silver, and green. *Metals:* gold, silver, and bronze. *Herbs:* lily and vervain.

Lakshmi (Hindu): The four-armed mother goddess who embodies all forms of wealth, generosity, and abundance. See chapter 4 for more information and a spell with Lakshmi. *Colors:* red and gold. *Metal:* Gold. *Semi-precious Stones:* ruby and pearl. *Herbs:* lotus and marigold.

Lugh (Celtic): A Celtic sun god, Lugh was the bountiful giver of the harvest. His festival day is August 1, or Lughnasadh. *Colors:* yellow, gold, and brown. *Metals:* bronze and gold. *Crystals:* sunstone and citrine. *Herbs:* blackberry, wheat, and grains.

Ra (Egypt): The Egyptian sun god, Ra was the embodiment of the sun in the sky and a god of birth and rebirth. He is a solar god to be called on for success and power. *Colors:* yellow and gold. *Metal:* gold. *Crystal:* lapis lazuli.

Zeus/Jupiter (Greco-Roman): The father god of the Greek and Roman pantheon and the god of the thunderbolt, the sky, and storms. Call on him for success, justice, and victory. Zeus/Jupiter is a powerhouse of energy and magick. He can grant wisdom, cunning, and prosperity if you approach him respectfully. *Colors:* white and gold. *Metal:* gold. *Crystal:* amber (I suggest the fossilized resin amber, as it is known to hold an electrical charge). *Herbs:* vervain, acorn, oak foliage, and wood.

A Group Prosperity Ritual

True prosperity is the result of well-placed
confidence in ourselves and our fellow man.

BENJAMIN BURT

Here is a prosperity ritual that you can work with your circle or coven. There may come a time when the whole group needs a little boost to their prosperity or is working for success and healthy abundance. This ritual calls upon four deities; one will be called at each of the quarters. They are complementary to prosperity work and magick in general. The basic instructions are here, but this ritual can certainly be personalized to your specific group's practices or tradition.

Timing: This spell is best worked on a waxing moon or on the night of a full moon.

Supplies: For flowers, use fresh yellow roses; for crystals and herbs, please see list of herbs and crystals from chapter 8 or in the second appendix. Also include gold coins (if possible), silver dimes, and wheat pennies. Add pictures of Ganesha, Lakshmi, Fortuna, and Juno Moneta.

   You can also include in your altar setup a few peacock feathers for Juno Moneta, the Wheel of the Year/Wheel of Fortune tarot card for Fortuna, and coins, marigolds, and sweets for Ganesha and Lakshmi.

Directions: Set up a pretty central altar devoted to prosperity magick. Cover the table with gold or green fabric. Tuck gold and green candles in a central cauldron—keeping them in a cauldron keeps the flames contained, especially important with an elaborately decorated altar. You can also put a sprinkling of golden magnetic sand at the bottom of the cauldron and set the candles on top of it.

You may need a large card table to arrange everything to your liking. Take your time and make the altar bewitching, attractive, and personal to your group. Have every member of the group bring items to contribute to the central altar. All of these images and items will help link the prosperity magick straight back to the coven/circle and their loved ones.

Once the altar is set up and the central candles are lit and flickering, gather in a circle around the altar and cast your ritual circle together.

Quarter Calls:

(EAST) *Fortuna, goddess of the wheel of the year and good luck,*
bring illumination and good fortune to us all.

(SOUTH) *Juno Moneta, great goddess and patron of the Roman mint,*
bless us always in the winter, spring, summer, and fall.

(WEST) *Lakshmi, dancing lady of spiritual wealth and joy,*
come into our lives and guide our hands and hearts.

(NORTH) *Loving Ganesha, remove all obstacles to our success,*
with care, bless us as we grow together in the magickal arts.

Casting the Ritual Circle: Start in the eastern quarter and have the first person take the hand of the person to their left and say:

Hand to hand I cast the circle.

Then the second person repeats this as they take the hand of the person to their left—and around the circle of members this goes, one at a time, until everyone has spoken the line and you have completely gone around clockwise. Once the last hand is clasped and you are all holding hands, then say in unison:

The circle is cast; we are between the worlds.

You may release hands. Next the prosperity spell verse is spoken. All members of the group should say this together.

Spell Verse:

We call upon Fortuna, Juno Moneta, Lakshmi, and Ganesha to combine their energies and bless us all with healthy abundance, success, and prosperity, both on a spiritual and a monetary level. May we experience all of your divine blessings in a positive and constructive way.

Fortuna, bless us with good luck and wisdom as we happily travel the wheel of the year. May your cornucopia flow freely, allowing magick to stream through our lives.

Juno Moneta, wise lady, may we learn to handle our finances cleverly; with your blessings, may our money increase and grow.

Lakshmi, dance into our lives and teach us to be rich on a spiritual level as well, for as we give generously to others, we do attract positive results back to ourselves.

Lord Ganesha, help us to remain encouraged as we face day-to-day challenges. Help us safely remove all obstacles in the path to our individual goals with grace.

We ask you all to help those gathered here to be successful, to stand in strength, and to travel our magickal path together. Let the teachings and practices of our coven bring illumination, joy, prosperity, and wisdom to us and to our loved ones in the best possible way.

Now raise energy as your group typically does. You may choose to spiral dance, hum, or clasp hands again and build the energy higher and higher. Once the energy has peaked, release it by tossing your hands up to the sky. Now all of the members should say together:

> *Our request is sincerely made, and now we close this verse,*
> *In no way can this magick turn or bring any curse.*

Sink to the earth and ground and center. After a bit of time has passed, share cakes and ale according to your own group's practices. While you are all chatting and relaxing, keep the conversation upbeat and positive; do not bring any talk of worries, want, or lack back into this ritual. When the cakes and ale are finished, stand up and release the quarters, this time starting in the north and moving to the left, or widdershins (counterclockwise):

> (NORTH) *Loving Ganesha, we thank you for your assistance,*
> *support, and for your loving strength. Blessed be.*

> (WEST) *Lakshmi, we thank you for your joyful presence*
> *in our lives and your generosity this night. Blessed be.*

> (SOUTH) *Juno Moneta, we thank you for your passion,*
> *grace, and the blessings of coins in our pockets. Blessed be.*

> (EARTH) *Fortuna, we thank you for the good fortune that*
> *you bring into our lives all the year long. Blessed be.*

Open the circle by saying the following as a group:

> *Ganesha, Lakshmi, Juno Moneta, and Fortuna,*
> *We thank you all! Hail and farewell.*
> *The circle is open but unbroken.*
> *Merry meet, merry part, and merry meet again!*

The ritual is finished. Divide up the fresh flowers and herbs between all who attended and let them take the floral components home to dry. (These botanicals are great to use in future prosperity charms and spells.) Clean up the rest of your altar setup before everyone heads home. Allow the candles in the cauldron to burn in a safe place until they go out on their own.

May your coven or circle be blessed.

Closing Thoughts

When you wish someone joy, you wish them peace,
love, prosperity, happiness…all the good things.

MAYA ANGELOU

This practical magick book took me longer to write than any other. But looking back, it all worked out as it should have. What began as a personal quest and a way to understand where I had gone wrong in my own prosperity spellcasting blossomed into a book filled with more advanced practices and deeper magick than I had originally planned.

This book took me on a magickal journey. It challenged what I thought I knew, and it taught me many wonderful things. My life has changed during the writing of this book, and the spiritual path that I have walked as the book took shape has been a fascinating one.

I hope you have enjoyed your time spent with me. It is my fondest wish that joy, happiness, prosperity, and peace will manifest in your lives. Be willing to work toward your goals on both the mundane and magickal planes, and I am sure you will be blessed with healthy abundance, success, and prosperity.

You can do it. I believe in you! Blessed be.

Appendix I

SPECIFIC-NEEDS
SPELL GUIDE

Success is focusing the full power of all you are
on what you have a burning desire to achieve.

WILFRED PETERSON

THE SPELLS IN this book were written with allowances for you to personalize them as you see fit. Also be sure to check the index or the table of contents for more spells, as not every spell in the book is suggested here. With this spell guide, you will find a quick reference for specific needs. The magickal need will be listed first, then the spell and chapter it is found in.

Staying Upbeat in Tough Times: A Floral Fascination to Reinforce a Positive Attitude (chapter 2)

Removing Negative Thoughtforms: Wind Chime Magick (chapter 2)

Success in New Ventures: Green Jar Candle Spell and Royal Blue Votive Candle Spell (chapter 3)

Spiritual Wealth and Fulfillment: A Spell for Prosperity with Lakshmi (chapter 4)

Spiritual Generosity/Generosity to Others: Calling on Yemaya for Success (chapter 4)

Wishes/Dreams Coming True: Nine of Cups Tarot Spell (chapter 4) and Bay Leaf Spell (p. 150)

Drawing Good Luck Quickly: Cornucopia Spell (chapter 5)

Drawing Money Quickly: Cornucopia Spell (chapter 5)

Good Luck: A Tarot Spell with Fortuna (chapter 5)

Attracting Health/Wealth and Fast Cash: Lodestone Witch-Jar Spell (chapter 5)

Attracting Good Luck: Lucky Cat Candle Spell (chapter 6)

Attracting New Customers: Empowering Your Cat Figurine (chapter 6)

Increasing Sales: Empowering Your Cat Figurine (chapter 6)

Removing Obstacles: Ganesha Spell (chapter 7) and The Tower Card Spell (chapter 7)

Removing Obstacles to Finding a Job: Ganesha Spell (chapter 7) and The Tower Card Spell (chapter 7)

Removing Spiritual Obstacles: The Tower Card Spell (chapter 7)

Help Applying to School or for Grants and Scholarships: Ganesha Spell (chapter 7)

General Magick for Merchants: Ganesha Spell (chapter 7)

Drawing Cash Quickly: Money Plant Spell (p. 153)

Transforming Bad Luck to Good: Tourmaline Spell (p. 161)

Giving Wealth and Joy to Another: Turquoise Spell (p. 163)

Personal Success: Sunrise Ritual (chapter 9)

Appendix II

HERBAL, CRYSTAL & METAL CORRESPONDENCES FOR PROSPERITY

Wealth is not a matter of intelligence,
it's a matter of inspiration.

JIM ROHN

Herbal Correspondences

Allspice: Mars

Beans: Mercury

Cedar: Sun

Chicory: Sun

Cinnamon: Sun

Cinquefoil: Jupiter

Clove: Jupiter

Clover: Mercury

Corn: Venus

Fig: Jupiter

Grapes: Moon

Heliotrope: Sun

Honeysuckle: Jupiter

Jasmine: Moon

Lotus: Moon

Maple: Jupiter

Mint: Pluto

Oak: Jupiter

Orange: Sun

Pine: Mars

Sunflower: Sun

Tulip: Venus

Crystal Correspondences

Agate, Dendritic: Mercury/earth. This stone of plenitude brings abundance to all areas, including business, gardening, and agriculture.

Agate, Moss: Mercury/earth. Attracts abundance and is a gardener's stone.

Aventurine: Mercury/air. A good luck stone often utilized in prosperity spells. A very positive stone of prosperity, it promotes a feeling of well-being.

Bloodstone: Mars/fire. A bloodstone kept in a cash register drawer will draw money. Carried in your pocket or purse, it will draw money.

Chrysoprase: Venus/earth. Promotes cheer as well as reduces envy, greed, and tension in a work environment. This pretty crystal also helps keep customers and employees loyal.

Citrine: Sun/fire. A stone of wealth and abundance, place it in the left corner of your home, farthest away from the front door, to attract wealth. Wearing citrine is a cleanser and an energizer; it boosts your motivation and makes you more creative, which in turn leads to prosperity.

Diamond: Sun/fire. A symbol of wealth, diamond amplifies energy. It's a stone of manifestation and it attracts abundance.

Emerald: Venus/earth. Use in business spells promoting sales and for publicity.

Jade: Venus/water. Wearing jade jewelry will help draw money into your life. It is also good for gardening.

Malachite: Venus/earth. Malachite placed in the corners of a business draws in customers; likewise if a small piece is placed in the cash register. Also helps promote a healthy garden.

Sapphire, Yellow: Moon/water. Attracts wealth to the home and business. Placed in cash register to increase sales. If worn, it should touch the body. Sacred to Ganesha.

Tiger's-eye: Sun/fire. Classically used to promote prosperity and cash. It is an energy-boosting, courageous stone, and it has protective attributes as well.

Topaz, Yellow: Sun/fire. Vital energy brings joy and abundance.

Tourmaline, Green: Venus/earth. This is used to draw money in as it is a receptive stone, excellent for gardening, and it boosts your creativity as well.

Turquoise: Venus, Neptune/earth. This stone can help success and prosperity to manifest in your life.

Metal Correspondences

Copper: Venus/water. Copper conducts electricity and is a lucky metal used to draw money, as in lucky pennies. Look for wheat pennies in particular. Copper is becoming increasingly popular in jewelry these days; look for pieces set with prosperity-inducing stones.

Gold: Sun/fire. Gold is a symbol of wealth and success. Wearing gold jewelry will increase your personal power. Gold coins work nicely for money magick.

Lodestone: Venus/water. Strengthens prosperity spells, as lodestones are all about attraction. To attract money or success in business, surround a lodestone with green candles.

Silver: Moon/water. Silver coins work especially well in prosperity and abundance spells. Watch for those silver Mercury dimes—check a coin store and look for a bargain.

GLOSSARY

Words are, in my not-so-humble opinion,
our most inexhaustible source of magic.

J. K. ROWLING

Amulet: A type of herbal charm, ornament, or jewel that aids and
protects its wearer. Amulets are passive; they do not project outward. They react to whatever is happening in the wearer's world.
See chapter 6.

Banishing: A magickal act that removes negativity or baneful
magick from your life.

Charge: To fill or imbue an object with magickal energy, such as
empowering spell candles. See chapter 3.

Charm: (1) A rhyming series of words or a simple spell used for
specific magickal purposes. (2) An object of magickal power such
as an amulet or talisman. (3) A small object worn on a bracelet or
chain. See chapter 6.

Charm Bag: Similar to a sachet, a charm bag is a small cloth bag
filled with herbs, charged crystals, and other magickal ingredients.

Circle: An informal group of Witches or Wiccans who study and
practice magick together.

Correspondences: A magickal classification system of interrela-
tions by which all things are categorized.

Coven: A group of Witches or Wiccans who practice magick together and worship together, with formalized rules, degree systems, training, and ritual practices.

Craft: The Witch's name for the Old Religion and the practice of Witchcraft.

Elements: The four natural elements are air, fire, water, and earth.

Enchantment: An act of magick. This word is often used interchangeably with the word *spell*.

Herb: A plant used for medicine, flavoring, food, or scent. Any part of the plant—the roots, stem, bark, leaves, seeds, or flowers—may be used for such purposes. An herb may be a tree, shrub, woody perennial, flower, annual, or fern.

Herbalism: Also known as herbal magick. The use of herbs in conjunction with magick to bring about positive change and transformation.

Hermetic Principles: The seven Hermetic principles are a set of philosophical beliefs based upon the ancient writings of Hermes Trismegistus. The Hermetic principles are like building blocks—they support one another—and the first principle is the foundation, with each principle supporting the next one. See chapter 1.

Law of Attraction: The law by which thought connects with its object—in this case, its objective. It enlightens us by showing that our thoughts are actual energy. Your thoughts manifest as vibrations, and that vibratory energy ripples out into the universe and becomes real. Thought creates! See chapter 1.

Magick: The combination of your own personal power that is used in harmony with natural objects such as herbs, crystals, and the elements. Once these are combined and your goal is focused upon, typically by the act of repeating a spell verse and lighting a candle or creating an herbal charm, the act of magick then creates a positive change.

Natural Magick: A style of magick that works in harmony with the various powers of the natural world and the four elements of earth, air, fire, and water.

Personal Magickal Energy (PME): Represents the amount of thought, effort, style, and power that you put into a prosperity spell when you first cast it. When you add up all those factors, you have a PME number. See chapter 7.

Rune: A sign or character in any of the runic futharks. Runes are figures from an ancient alphabet that are used as a divinatory system, and the symbols are often used in spellcraft.

Spell: A series of rhyming words that verbally announces the spellcaster's intention. When these spoken words are combined with specific actions such as lighting a candle, creating an amulet, or gathering an herb, this is then worked in harmony with the tides of nature and, combined with the spellcaster's personal energy, endows the magickal act with the power to create positive change.

Talisman: An object created from any type of material with a specific goal in mind such as increasing power or bestowing extra protection. See chapter 6.

Thaumaturgy: The use of magickal powers to influence or predict events. It can be defined as Witchcraft or conjuration. This type of magick is earthy and simple. It relies on the use of natural items. Practices like herb magick, crystal magick, candle magick, and sympathetic magick may be called low magick or, more correctly, practical magick.

Theurgy: Rituals that are designed to align oneself with the Divine or the angelic realms. Theurgy, also known as high magick, is a type of magickal practice that has its emphasis placed on more spiritual goals and communing directly with the Divine. High magick often incorporates mathematics, astrology, alchemy, and the Kabbalah.

Thoughtforms: Thoughtforms are created by strong positive thoughts or intense negative thoughts that then take on a life of their own and exist on the astral plane.

Wicca: A Neopagan earth religion. Its followers generally believe in harming no one with their magick. Wiccans follow and celebrate the seasons and cycles of the year, and see the Divine as both masculine and feminine.

Witch: A practitioner of magick. A Witch may not necessarily be a Wiccan. That being said, most Witches will work their magick from a place of neutrality. Witches know and accept that they are fully accountable and responsible for all of their actions on both mundane and magickal levels.

BIBLIOGRAPHY

*Books let us into their souls and
lay open to us the secrets of our own.*

WILLIAM HAZLITT

Adams, Anton, and Mina Adams. *The Learned Art of Witches &
Wizards*. New York: Barnes & Noble Books, 2000.

Ahlquist, Diane. *The Complete Idiot's Guide to the Law of Attraction*.
New York: Penguin, 2008.

Ban Breathnach, Sarah. *Simple Abundance: A Daybook of Comfort
and Joy*. New York: Warner Books, 1995.

————. *Peace and Plenty: Finding Your Path to Financial Serenity*.
New York: Grand Central Publishing, 2010.

Bonewits, Issac. *Real Magic*. Boston, MA: Red Wheel/Weiser, 1989.

Bowes, Susan. *Notions and Potions*. New York: Sterling, 1997.

Bren, Marion Luna. *The 7 Greatest Truths about Successful Women*.
New York: G. P. Putnam's Sons, 2001.

Byrne, Rhonda. *The Secret*. New York: Atria Books, 2006.

Cabot, Laurie, and Tom Cowan. *Power of the Witch*. New York: Dell
Publishing, 1989.

Chopra, Deepak. *The 7 Spiritual Laws of Success.* San Rafael, CA: Amber-Allen Publishing, 1994.

Chu, Ernest D. *Soul Currency: Investing Your Inner Wealth for Fulfillment & Abundance.* Novato, CA: New World Library, 2008.

Cole-Whittaker, Terry. *Live Your Bliss.* Novato, CA: New World Library, 2009.

Cunningham, Scott. *Cunningham's Encyclopedia of Magical Herbs.* St. Paul, MN: Llewellyn, 1996.

Demarco, Stacey. *Witch in the Boardroom.* Woodbury, MN: Llewellyn, 2005.

Dugan, Ellen. *Book of Witchery.* Woodbury, MN: Llewellyn, 2009.

———. "Charmed Jewelry," 2014 *Witches Datebook* article. Woodbury, MN: Llewellyn, 2013.

———. *Cottage Witchery.* St. Paul, MN: Llewellyn, 2005.

———. *Garden Witch's Herbal.* Woodbury, MN: Llewellyn, 2009.

———. *Herb Magic for Beginners.* Woodbury, MN: Llewellyn, 2006.

———. *How to Enchant a Man.* Woodbury, MN: Llewellyn, 2008.

———. "Lakshmi," 2014 *Magical Almanac* article. Woodbury, MN: Llewellyn, 2013.

———. "September," 2013 *Witches Calendar* article. Woodbury, MN: Llewellyn, 2012.

———. *Practical Protection Magick.* Woodbury, MN: Llewellyn, 2011.

———. *The Enchanted Cat.* Woodbury, MN: Llewellyn, 2006.

———. *Witches Tarot Companion.* Woodbury, MN: Llewellyn, 2012.

Farrar, Janet, and Stewart Farrar. *Spells & How They Work*. Custer, WA: Phoenix Publishing, 1990.

Gallagher, Anne-Marie. *The Spells Bible*. Cincinnati: Walking Stick Press, 2003.

Grant, Ember. "The Three R's of Chant Writing," 2011 *Magical Almanac* article. Woodbury, MN: Llewellyn, 2011.

———. *Magical Candle Crafting*. Woodbury, MN: Llewellyn, 2011.

Hall, Judy. *The Crystal Bible*. Cincinnati: Walking Stick Press, 2003.

Illes, Judika. *The Element Encyclopedia of 5000 Spells*. London: HarperElement, 2004.

———. *The Element Encyclopedia of Witchcraft*. London: HarperElement, 2005.

Katz, Debra Lynne. *Freeing the Genie Within*. Woodbury, MN: Llewellyn, 2009.

Killion, Cynthia. *A Little Book of Prosperity Magic*. Freedom, CA: Crossing Press, 2001.

The Kybalion. Hollister, MO: YOG eBooks by Roger L. Cole, 2010.

Losier, Michael, J. *Law of Attraction*. Victoria, BC: Wellness Central, 2010.

Marquis, Melanie. *The Witch's Bag of Tricks*. Woodbury, MN: Llewellyn, 2011.

Pattanail, Devdutt. *Lakshmi: Goddess of Wealth and Fortune: An Introduction*. Mumbai, India: Vakils, Feffer and Simons Private Ltd., 2002.

Penczak, Christopher. *The Inner Temple of Witchcraft*. St. Paul, MN: Llewellyn, 2003.

———. *The Outer Temple of Witchcraft*. St. Paul, MN: Llewellyn, 2004.

———. *The Temple of High Witchcraft*. Woodbury, MN: Llewellyn, 2007.

———. *The Witch's Coin*. Woodbury, MN: Llewellyn, 2009.

Pollack, Rachel. *Tarot Wisdom*. Woodbury, MN: Llewellyn, 2008.

Ravenwolf, Silver. *Silver's Spells for Prosperity*. St. Paul, MN: Llewellyn, 1999.

Roman, Sanaya, and Duane Packer. *Creating Money: Attracting Abundance*. Tiburon, CA: New World Library, 2008.

Telesco, Patricia. *Money Magick*. Franklin Lakes, NJ: New Page, 2001.

Trobe, Kala. *Invoke the Goddess*. St. Paul, MN: Llewellyn, 2000.

———. *The Witch's Guide to Life*. St. Paul, MN: Llewellyn, 2003.

Weatherford, Jack. *The History of Money*. New York: Crown Publishers, 1997.

Webster, Richard. *Amulets and Talismans for Beginners*. St. Paul, MN: Llewellyn, 2004.

Whitehurst, Tess. *Magical Housekeeping*. Woodbury, MN: Llewellyn, 2010.

———. *The Art of Bliss*. Woodbury, MN: Llewellyn, 2012.

INDEX

GET MORE AT LLEWELLYN.COM

Visit us online to browse hundreds of our books and decks, plus sign up to receive our e-newsletters and exclusive online offers.

- • Free tarot readings • Spell-a-Day • Moon phases
- • Recipes, spells, and tips • Blogs • Encyclopedia
- • Author interviews, articles, and upcoming events

GET SOCIAL WITH LLEWELLYN

Find us on

www.Facebook.com/LlewellynBooks

Follow us on

www.Twitter.com/Llewellynbooks

GET BOOKS AT LLEWELLYN

LLEWELLYN ORDERING INFORMATION

Order online: Visit our website at www.llewellyn.com to select your books and place an order on our secure server.

Order by phone:
- • Call toll free within the U.S. at 1-877-NEW-WRLD (1-877-639-9753)
- • Call toll free within Canada at 1-866-NEW-WRLD (1-866-639-9753)
- • We accept VISA, MasterCard, and American Express

Order by mail:
Send the full price of your order (MN residents add 6.875% sales tax) in U.S. funds, plus postage and handling to: Llewellyn Worldwide, 2143 Wooddale Drive Woodbury, MN 55125-2989

POSTAGE AND HANDLING

STANDARD (U.S. & Canada):
(Please allow 12 business days)
$25.00 and under, add $4.00.
$25.01 and over, FREE SHIPPING.

INTERNATIONAL ORDERS (airmail only):
$16.00 for one book, plus $3.00 for each additional book.

Visit us online for more shipping options. Prices subject to change.

FREE CATALOG!

To order, call
1-877-
NEW-WRLD
ext. 8236
or visit our
website

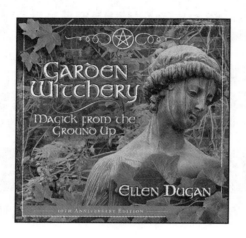

To order, call 1-877-NEW-WRLD

Prices subject to change without notice

Order at llewellyn.com 24 hours a day, 7 days a week!

Garden Witchery
Magick from the Ground Up

Ellen Dugan

How does your magickal garden grow? Garden Witchery is more than belladonna and wolfsbane. It's about making your own enchanted backyard with the trees, flowers, and plants found growing around you. It's about creating your own flower fascinations and spells, and it's full of common-sense information about cold hardiness zones, soil requirements, and a realistic listing of accessible magickal plants.

There may be other books on magickal gardening, but none have practical gardening advice, magickal correspondences, flower folklore, moon gardening, faery magick, advanced Witchcraft, and humorous personal anecdotes all rolled into one volume. *Garden Witchery* is now available in a tenth anniversary edition. Includes a gardening journal.

978-0-7387-0318-3
7½ x 7½ • 304 pp.

COTTAGE WITCHERY

NATURAL MAGICK FOR HEARTH AND HOME

ELLEN DUGAN

To order, call 1-877-NEW-WRLD

Prices subject to change without notice

Order at llewellyn.com 24 hours a day, 7 days a week!

Cottage Witchery
Natural Magick for Hearth and Home

Ellen Dugan

There's no place like a magickal home and Ellen Dugan, the author of *Garden Witchery*, is the ideal guide to show us how to bring the beauty of nature and its magickal energies indoors. Using common household and outdoor items—such as herbs, spices, dried flowers, plants, stones, and candles—she offers a down-to-earth approach to creating an enchanted home.

From specialized spells and charms to kitchen conjuring and color magick, this hands-on guide teaches Witches of all levels how to strengthen a home's aura and energy. Readers will learn how to use begonias and lilacs for protection, dispel bad vibes with salt and lemon, perform tea leaf readings, bless the home with fruit, invite the help of faeries, perform houseplant magick, and create a loving home for the whole family.

978-0-7387-0625-2
7½ x 7½ • 288 pp.

To order, call 1-877-NEW-WRLD

Prices subject to change without notice

Order at llewellyn.com 24 hours a day, 7 days a week!

Seasons of Witchery
*Celebrating the Sabbats
with the Garden Witch*

Ellen Dugan

In *Seasons of Witchery*, the newest release in Ellen Dugan's best-selling series, she offers readers a wealth of magickal ways to celebrate the wheel of the year. With her trademark warmth and practicality, Ellen shares a bit of history and lore on each sabbat as well as simple yet meaningful ideas for honoring each season. There are colorful decorating suggestions, fun craft projects, tasty recipes, insightful journal notes about her enchanted garden through the year, and natural magick aligned with each holiday. This charming and friendly book will inspire readers with new ideas, fresh spells, and seasonal rituals to make their own sabbat celebrations more personal and powerful.

978-0-7387-3078-3
7½ x 7½ • 336 pp.

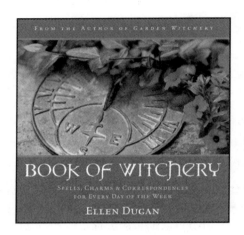

To order, call 1-877-NEW-WRLD

Prices subject to change without notice

Order at llewellyn.com 24 hours a day, 7 days a week!

Book of Witchery
Spells, Charms & Correspondences
for Every Day of the Week

Ellen Dugan

Kick-start your magickal creativity and incorporate the Craft into your everyday life. Award-winning author Ellen Dugan offers many fresh ideas on building your own personal style of witchery, so you can happily conjure seven days a week. This friendly guide will help you learn the fundamentals and make good use of the magickal energies each day holds. Formerly available as *7 Days of Magic*, this treasury of Witchcraft essentials has more than doubled in size and features a wealth of brand-new material.

978-0-7387-1584-1
7½ x 7½ • 360 pp.

To order, call 1-877-NEW-WRLD

Prices subject to change without notice

Order at llewellyn.com 24 hours a day, 7 days a week!

Practical Protection Magick
Guarding & Reclaiming Your Power
Ellen Dugan

Embrace your inner warrior to safeguard your personal power. Use protection magick and psychic self-defense to stay strong, healthy, and happy.

With honesty and humor, best-selling author Ellen Dugan teaches how to weave safe and sensible protection magick into your practice and daily life. This unique practical guide reveals how to pinpoint your psychic strengths, set boundaries, diagnose a problem with divination, and maintain health on physical, psychic, and magickal levels. You'll also find simple and potent spells, rituals, and warding techniques to defend against psychic attacks, emotional and psychic vampires, hexes, unwanted ghosts, and other forms of negativity threatening your home and your well-being.

978-0-7387-2168-2
6 x 9, 240 pp.

To order, call 1-877-NEW-WRLD

Prices subject to change without notice

Order at llewellyn.com 24 hours a day, 7 days a week!

Witches Tarot
Illustrated by Mark Evans

Ellen Dugan

Witches the world over will relish this new tarot! Award-winning author Ellen Dugan, a highly respected Witch and tarot reader, and award-winning artist Mark Evans have created the perfect deck for all devotees of the Craft.

Positively radiating witchy energy, this easy-to-use tarot showcases beautiful and evocative digital artwork. Echoing the traditional Rider-Waite structure, each card includes instantly recognizable Pagan symbols that resonate with today's Witch. In addition to card descriptions and meanings, Dugan's companion guide features seven unique, spell-enhancing spreads for both tarot readings and magickal practice.

978-0-7387-2800-1
kit includes 312-pp. book and 78-card deck

To Write to the Author

If you wish to contact the author or would like more information about this book, please write to the author in care of Llewellyn Worldwide and we will forward your request. Both the author and the publisher appreciate hearing from you and learning of your enjoyment of this book and how it has helped you. Llewellyn Worldwide cannot guarantee that every letter written to the author can be answered, but all will be forwarded. Please write to:

Ellen Dugan
℅ Llewellyn Worldwide
2143 Wooddale Drive
Woodbury, MN 55125-2989

Please enclose a self-addressed stamped envelope for reply
or $1.00 to cover costs. If outside the USA, enclose
an international postal reply coupon.

Many of Llewellyn's authors have websites with additional information and resources. For more information, please visit our website:

WWW.LLEWELLYN.COM

good words

by Mark Levinson
& Élise Hannebicque

The Paris Savannah Company
www.goodwords.us

The Paris Savannah Company
Published by The Paris Savannah Company
4 square Henry Paté 75016 Paris, France.

First published in 2015 by
The Paris Savannah Company

ISBN 979-10-95151-00-5
EAN 9791095151

Text by Mark Levinson and graphics by Elise Hannebicque.

The paper in this book meets the guidelines for
performance and durability of the Committee on
Production Guidelines for Book Longevity of the Counsel
of Library Services.

Printed and bound in the Czech Republic
Dépot légal (France) Octobre 2015

To my father,
Eugene Leonard Levinson who
always used to say:

" If you can't say something good
about someone...

...don't say it! "

and to Eunice Ginsberg, mother of 4 who could sum up just about any situation with a proverb, quote or saying a few of which you'll find on these pages and not the least of which must have had a Freudian overtone:

" Necessity is the mother of invention. "

and to this chaotic group of wonderful, unique friends and family,

arnoul and daphné and pierre and jacqueline and michel and ruby and joseph and gabriele and henrik and isabelle and emma and reuben and florence and karyn and fanny and sue and vincent and claudine and haïm and helen and shoshanna and jean-pierre and elise and melinda and luc and colette and tom and lucille and steve and nathan and sharyn and caroline and bernard and lucy lea and françois and noah and serge and gail and jean and katherine and issac and garance and dick and gérard and juliette anna and raphael and david and barbara and mathias and amaia and ben and joe and sherry and myron and lucia and danielle and babé and manny and justin and anne and jay conrad and micayla and bea and cyril and suzanne and pamela and yayoi and jack and sonia and ronnie and laure and rami and dobbie and antonio and léoncie and arbro and judy and jean-robert and roopin and neili and filmore and stella and emily and patrick and eliane and jacques and mark and tiphaine and paul and aurélie and benjamin and susan and moshe and linda and manu and cécile and sammy and justine and oscar and rosemary and fabien and etienne and agathe and dominique and stanley and paula and mireille and omer and pascal and marie and john and sharry and laurent and martine and augustin and rachel and deyi and eliot and lauriane and jean-christophe and betsy and héloise and niranjan and sarah and jeremy and anne-claire and marcello and gina and grégoire and rita and anne-marie and howard and emilie and sushil and corinne and jason and leah and cornelia and leigh and gilles and alexandra and ruth and abe and deborah and louis and doris and marty and elana and laurence and arthur and emmanuelle and eric and julie and solomon and kay and leonora and jennifer and avrom and xavier and rob and harriet and giulia and susie and nathalie and diego and laura and maxence and gisela and craig and valdina and marc and pascaline and jean-yves and harvey and théotine and pauline and géraldine and ronna and chantal and eva and rochelle and jeanne and sylvia and april and emmanuel and leonardo and kalia and shiraz and fannie and sophie and clara and erin and jean-jacques and marjorie and charles and ada and bobby and maria helena and romain and sammy and brune and fred and pascale and alexis and bérénice and mickey and nate and janine and edith and vivian and peggy and thomas and chloé and shari and mathieu and denise and david and valérie and ella and quentin and george and mathew and phillip and jean-baptiste and mary and ishtar and ruthie and flore and achille and laure-anaïs and fabienne and catherine and jean-louis and racquel and rose and stanford and marion and pierre-yves and karen and rodger and alexia and marvin and sarianna and ida and léopoldine and karine and robert and delphine and clémence and bruno and sydney and icrame and norman and minnie and rebecca and léonard and aurelien and marie-christine and monique and tristan and rusty and bob and evelyne and robin and coralie and renée and mccall and louise and carole and choqui and eve and dorothée and freda and jean-noel and sebastien and charlene and geoff and ophélie and juli and thierry and adam and william and gabriella and emeric and rasmus and tanya and elvira and dorothy and nitza and jake and martin and aneta and yoav and salima and alex and claire and neil and jon and gloria and quentin and joan and olivier and eleonore and bill and judith and margaux and jérome and veronique and johan and lem and jeannie and mario and amy and nolan and esther and françoise and sarah and stéphanie and didier and béatrice and nicolas and arié and bruce and jill and jean-marc and marine and léonid and aude and josh and lilach and gabriel and helena and jelena and harold and miriam and kathleen and marcel and david and enoch and joseph and shyam and maurice and vera and micah and giovanni and moise and claude and christine and bar and claudette and james and carita and brian and pramod and annette and christophe and yulia and daniel and ram and alain and annie and jean-paul and jane and francine...

and all of those, too, whom I haven't mentionned but who are so, so special and are, in my book, not only good names but even moreso, good people

to you!

Good words are those which carry us up! Those that bring smiles to our faces like a bouquet of spring flowers or the melody of a loved, familiar tune.
They're the understanding expression you sense from a newfound friend!

Good words bring out the best in us: appreciation, hope and enthusiasm, trust and dignity.
They are the thankyou we offer to others, to ourselves.
They are expressions of joy and gratitude and surprise; good words are sincere and encouraging. Pleasing to the ear and to the eye, good words are dialogue.

Good words are feelgood words like the feeling
of a gentle breeze on a summer day or the warmth and
coziness at home on an autumn evening.

Good words are all those we live as we use our hearts,
our souls and our minds all together! They carry us from
project to project looking optimistically to the future in
calm confidence.

Good words bring color into our lives, stimulating our
imaginations and opening us to insights into our worlds.

Words carry deep, powerful meanings. They are messages coded in sound, rooted like old, live oak trees in history. The vast majortity of our words were here before us and will still be here long after we're gone but it is us, now, who give them life.

Each spoken word is a breath of life. The power of the single word travels far both in time and space for it can be repeated uniquely at will by each and every one of us with our own special voices. Our voices have our own picthes and tones; our own personalities which breathe meanings into words, making them, for a time, our own.

As every performer knows, each word can be spoken softly, loudly, with compassion, emotion slowly or quickly. Whispered. If the picture is, as we say, worth a thousand words, a good word is worth a beautiful day.

Good words lighten our hearts, please our senses, bring smiles to our faces, show appreciation and gratitude. Good words make our days beautiful.

The 365 words on the following pages are yours. Like your smile, limitless in the joy they bring you and those you care for. Use them in the morning, use them in the afternoon, evening and at night. Use them in the spring, summer, autumn and winter. Say kind words to hear kind words !

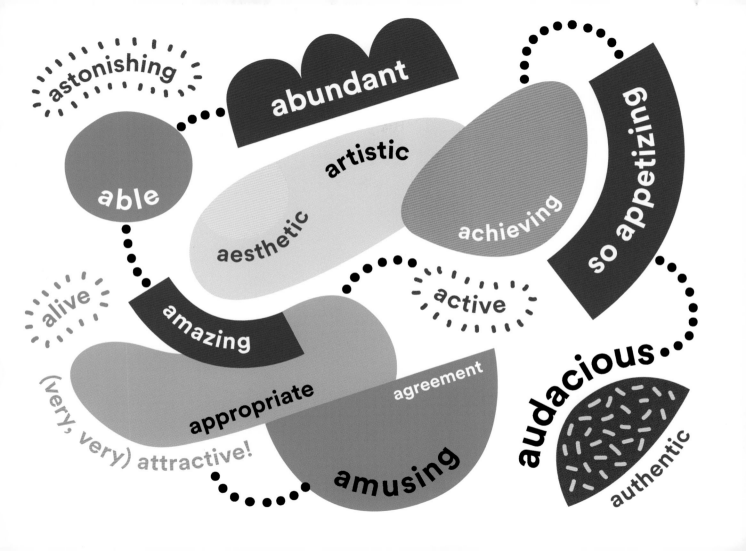

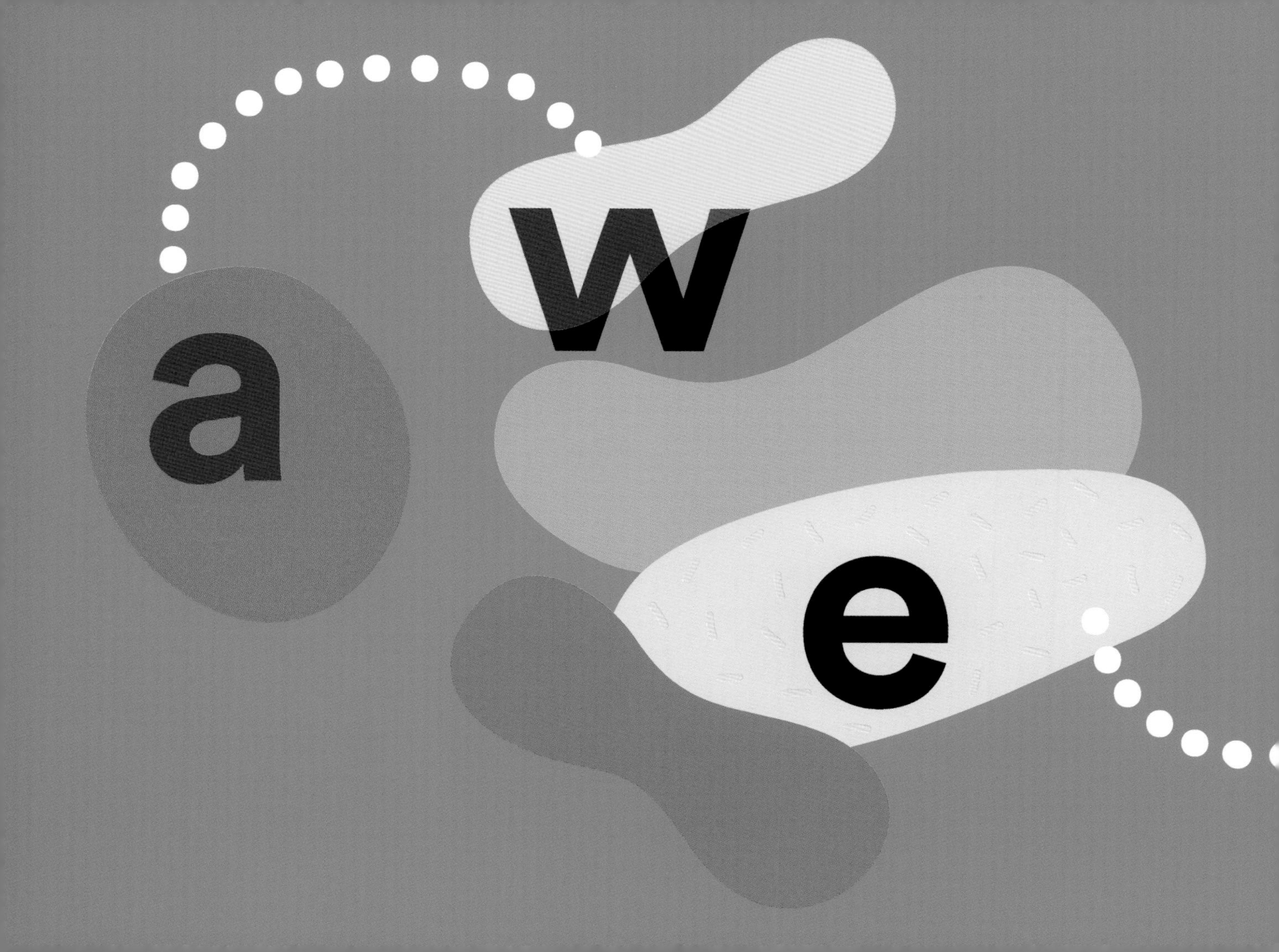
a
w
e

some

An apple a day keeps

the doctor away

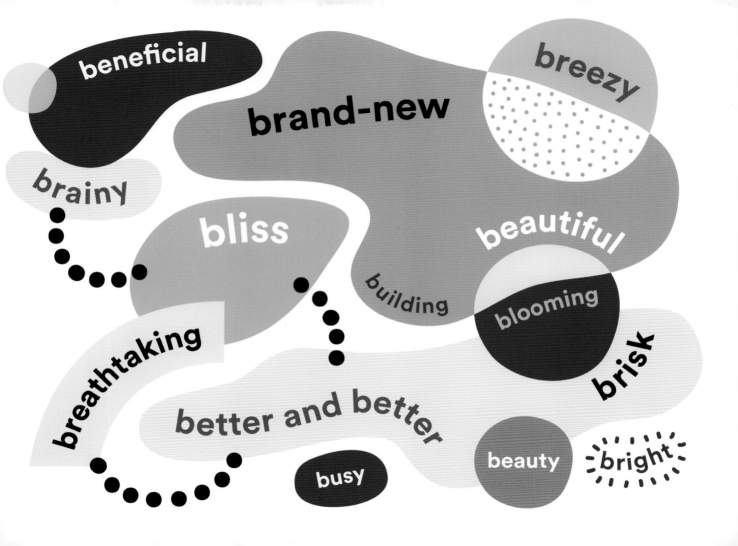

Beauty is in the eye

of the beholder.

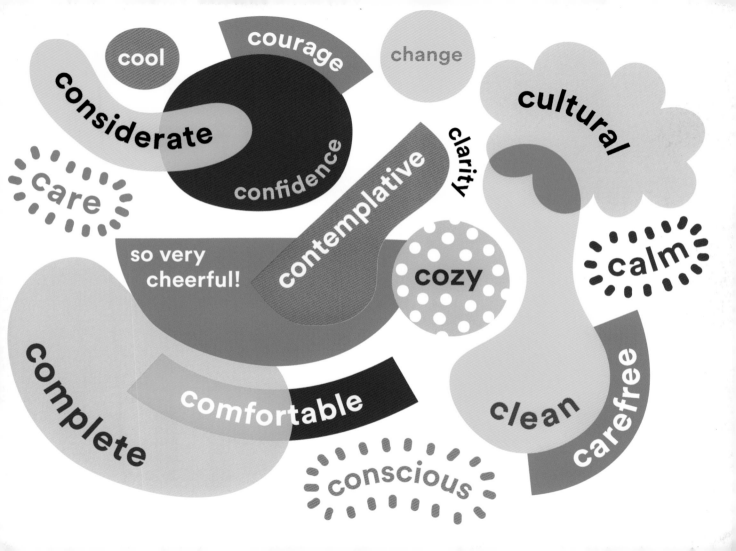

colorful

too ...

Cleanliness is next

to Godliness.

If it weren't for the
we wouldn't know
or dusk.

night,
dawn, daylight

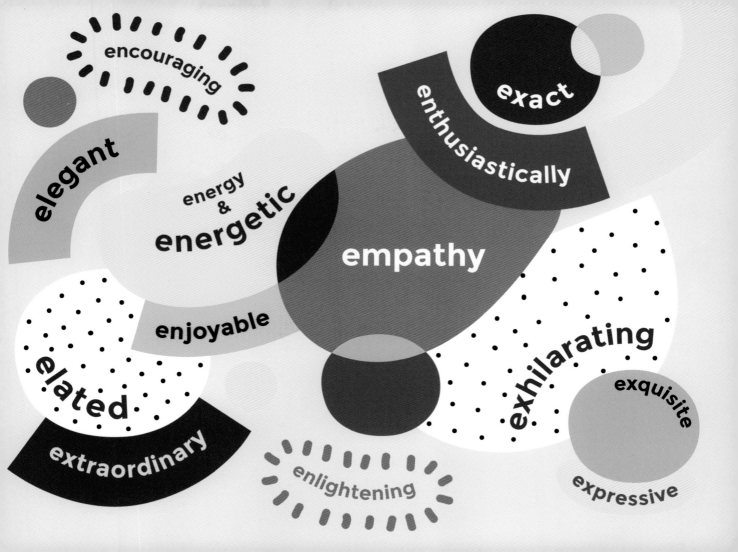

tional!!

The early bird

catches the worm.

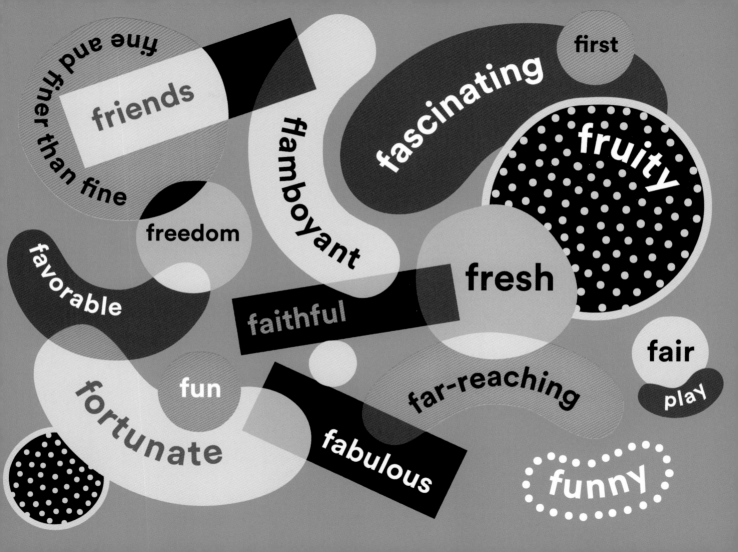

Friends of friends of

friends

are our friends

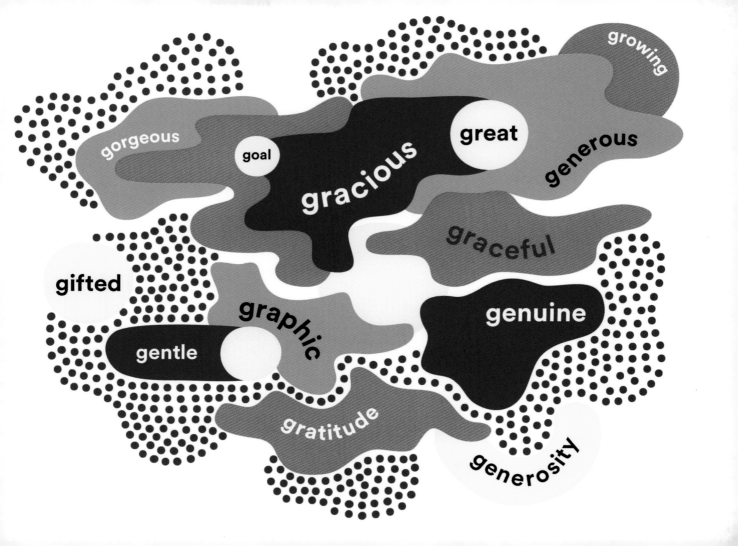

Good morning!

Good evening!

Good going!

Good work!

Good timing!

Good afternoon!

Goodwill

Good luck!

Good night...

Great minds

Home **is where**

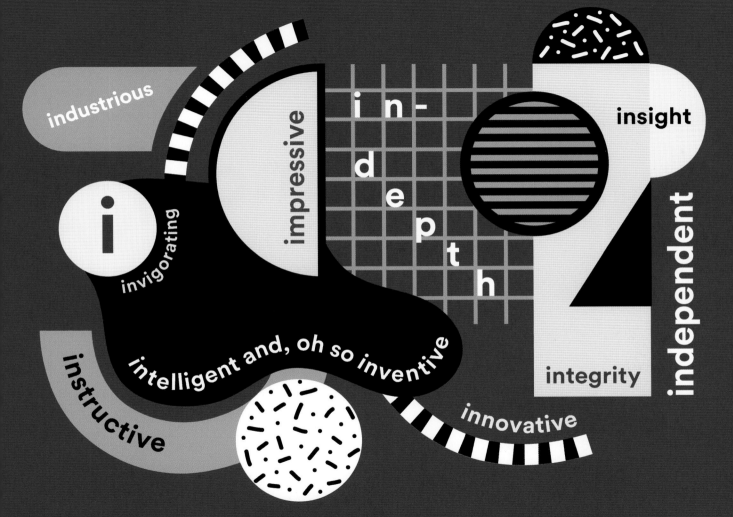

Necessity is the mother

of invention.

Many a true word

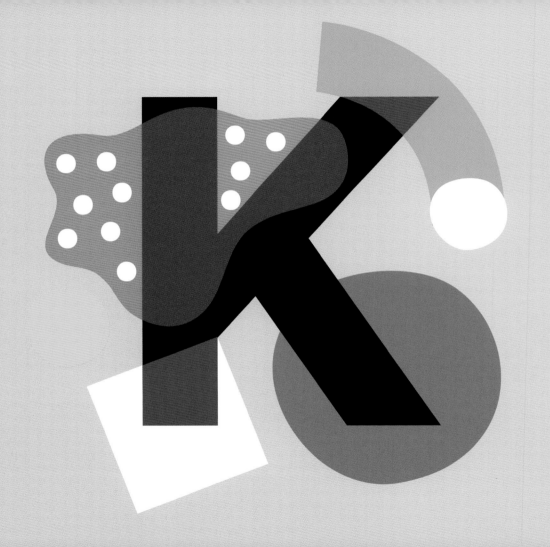

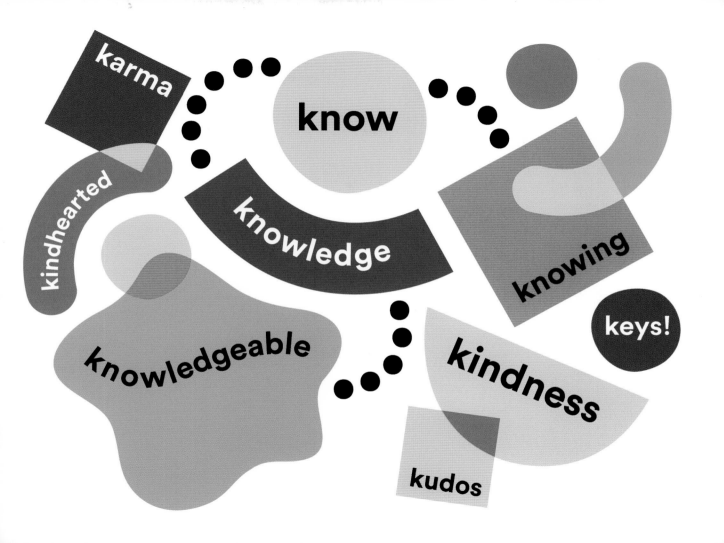

Say
kind words

to hear

kind words.

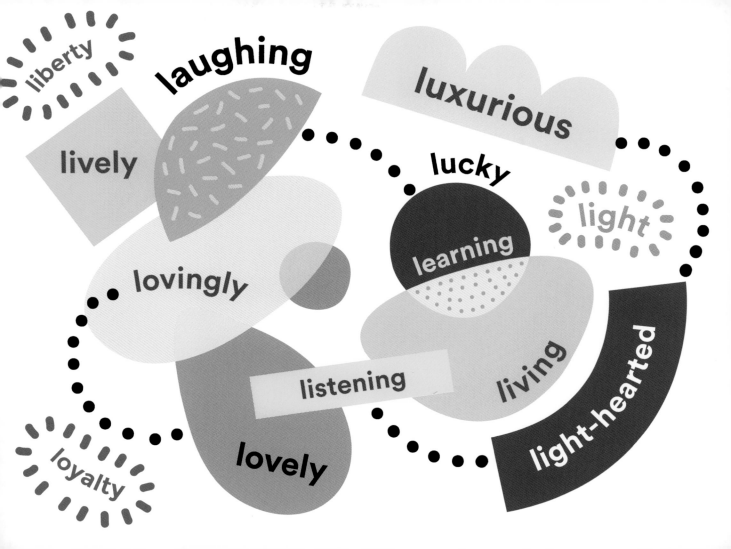

Love will

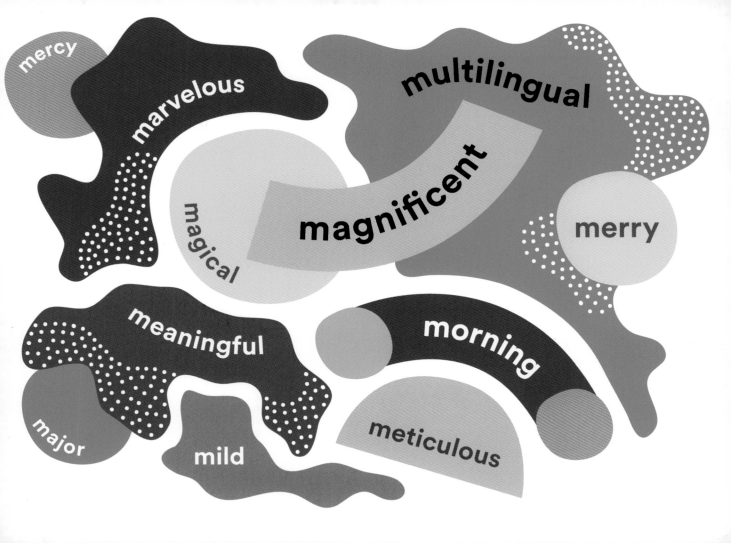

Make hay while

the sun shines

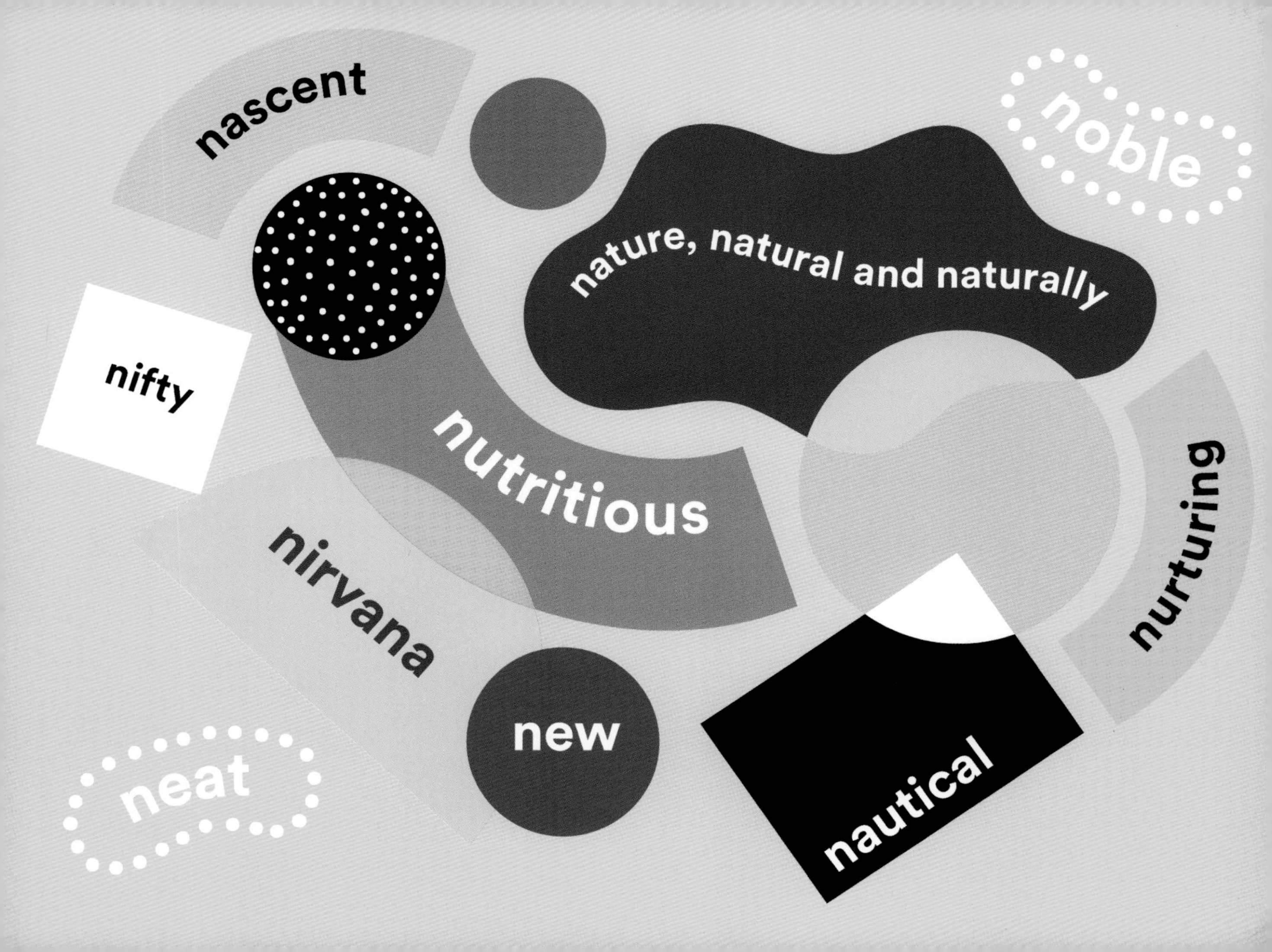

nascent

noble

nature, natural and naturally

nifty

nutritious

nurturing

nirvana

new

neat

nautical

very nice

how nice of you!

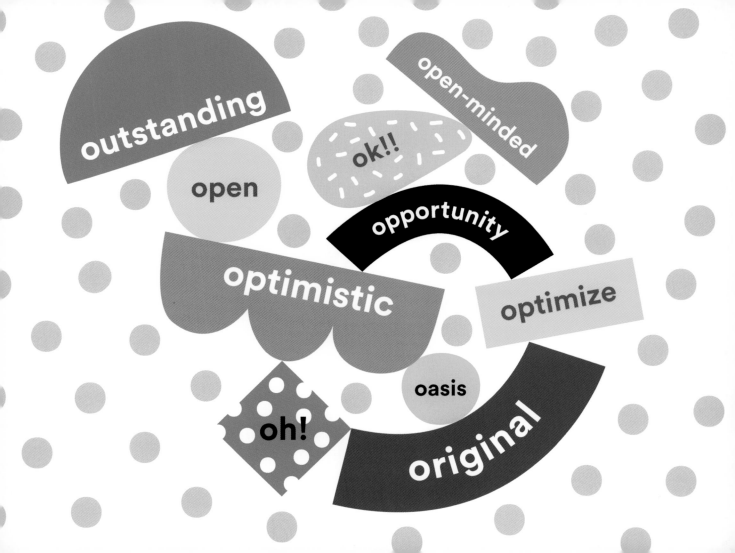

Every owl has

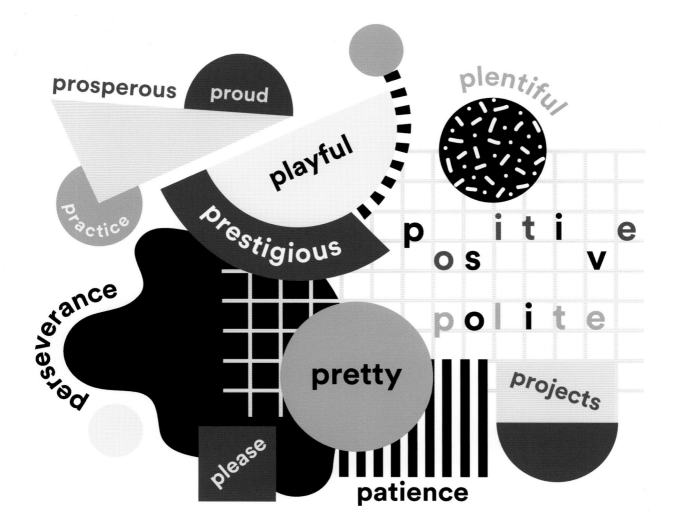

Practice

makes perfect!

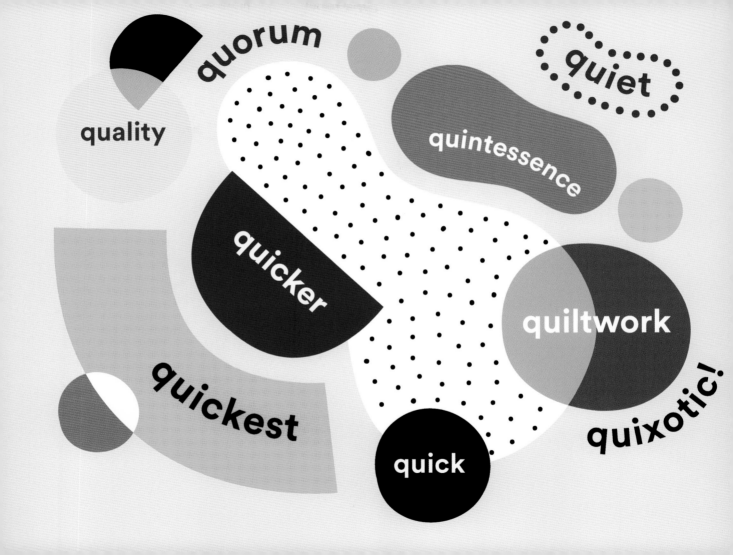

as a silly question.

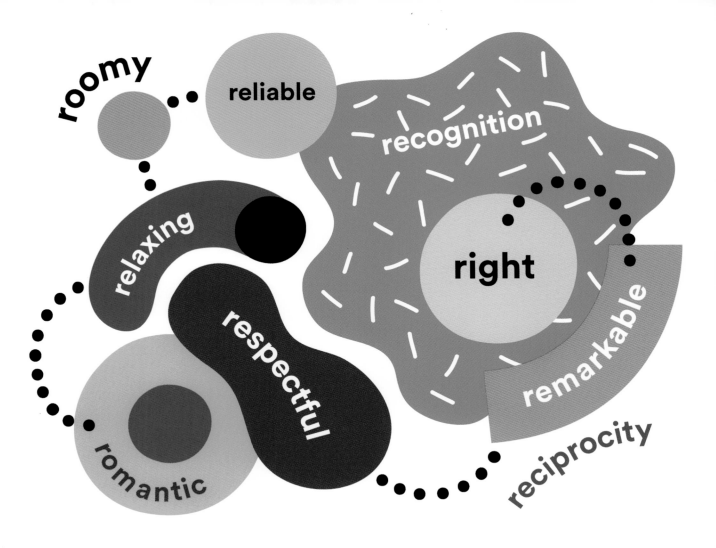

Rolling stones

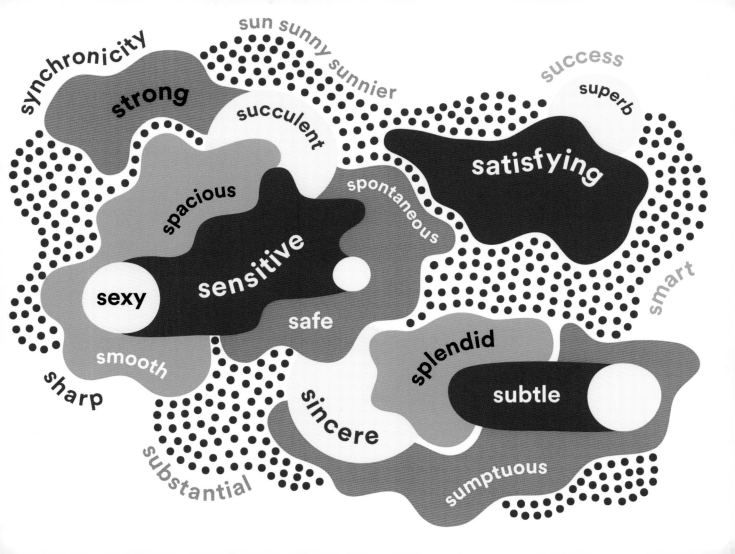

than sorry!

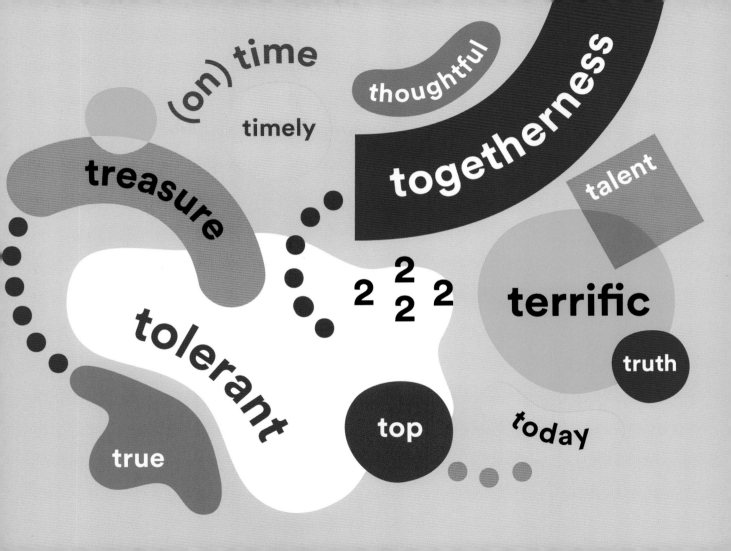

Two heads are

United

we stand.

Variety is the

spice of life!

Where there's a will,

there's a way

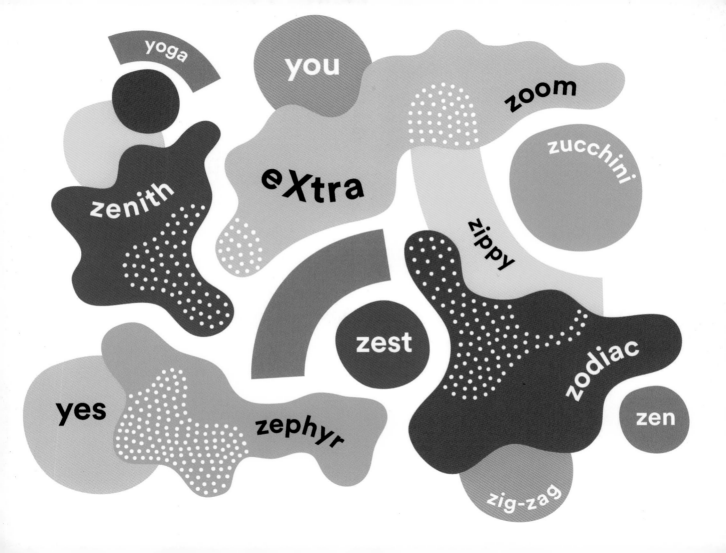

And … a few words about proverbs!
My father also used to say: « A word to the wise is
sufficient. » Where did he learn this? From his parents?
From a teacher? From a friend? From my mother?
What's important is that those old words, put together,
were spoken by one, understood by the other and kept, like
jewels in a jewelry box in the mind to be taken out
and spoken just at the right time and right place. Shared
in the hope that they would help us be better people if they
made some sense to us. They might have been a strong
suggestion, maybe a warning! Nonetheless, they
made sense and I learned that they could be applied
to many a new situation, too.

Such is the enduring life of proverbs. Short, concise, to the point, they pass from person-to-person in the present. In the course of time, from one generation to the next and then into the future. Sometimes they seem to fall asleep for a hundred years like Rip Van Winkle and then wake up again!

Good words. Because they are true.
And that's a good word!

Mark Levinson

Teacher. Translator. Proofreader. Linguist. Author. Speechwriter. Co-chair of the Education and Training Committee at AmCham France and founder of the Paris Savannah Company, Mark works with a variety of professionals in advertising and design, students, artists, as well as scientists.

His passion for excellence in language led to the creation of this unique collection of GOOD WORDS and the present graphic creation with Elise.

Elise Hannebicque

Elise is a young Parisian graphic artist and illustrator with a passion for working with shapes and colors, often textile and texture inspired.
The important thing is the handmade and even when working in a digital medium, her process is always instinctive and manual. There's nothing automatic or preprogrammed in Elise's creation.

that ends well.